THE

FERGUSON ALBUM

Allan T. Condie

Title Page: The Georgian Baroque of Stoneleigh Abbey, designed by Francis Smith of Warwick and the 'thirties style of the Fergie 20 make a perfect picture.

CONTENTS

ISBN 0 907742 82 3 Hardback   ISBN 0 907742 83 1 Softback

Design, Layout and Editing by Allan T Condie.
Typesetting, Photo reproduction, and Printing by Elgar Printing Ltd., Hereford.

Allan T. Condie Publications, 40 Main Street, Carlton, NUNEATON. CV13 ORG.
Telephone 0455-290389.

Right: Harry Ferguson.

PREFACE

In 1986 a picture album called "The New Ferguson Album" was launched as the first of a new series from this publisher.

So successful has this title been, that after two printings, it has sold out again.

The enthusiasm within the Massey Ferguson organisation for the original book has brought about this new edition, with many more illustrations added, and the story brought more up to date - to the mid seventies in fact.

Although the gambit has been to retain the flavour of the original book, the text has been completely revised in the light of further research, and background history on the two other constituents of Massey Ferguson, Massey Harris and F. Perkins of Peterborough added.

Allan T. Condie.   *Carlton, July 1990*

ACKNOWLEDGEMENTS

Firstly, thanks must go to Colin Booth who helped with the original book on Ferguson, and on whose footings this present edition has been built. Other individuals who have helped are Charles Cawood, John Melloy, Mervyn Spokes, Bill Martin, and Dereck Lambe.

In the M-F organisation, thanks must go to Jim Newbold and Graham Black for opening the way to the creation of a much better 'new edition'. Their introduction to Ted Everett, who has been in the photographic department for many years, has resulted in finding many new and interesting shots for this album, including the splendid colour ones on the cover. The photographic department at Perkins in Peterborough, in the persons of Lionel Chandler and Clive Scattergood, has provided pictures to illustrate things from the 'engine' angle, and Bill Martin from Ulster has filled in the gaps on the early days and the Ford-Ferguson scene, whilst those for the type 'A' have come from the Museum of English Rural Life.

Chapter One
Beginnings

In 1919 Harry Ferguson found himself working for the Irish Board of Agriculture. He became involved in a scheme to improve the efficiency of tractor use in Ireland.

He came to the conclusion that the main problem that existed at that time was the complicated design and construction of the ploughs and the tractors, which although extremely crude and heavy were relatively simple to operate and maintain. When the job was over he decided that he could design a plough far superior to any then in production.

The tractors which Ferguson had most experience of were International Titan and Mogul models, heavy and complex machines, but when Ferguson turned to building his first mechanically operated mounted plough he fitted this to an 'Eros' conversion on the Ford model 'T' car.

This plough was of simple two furrow design mounted on the rear of the tractor, with balance springs so that it could be easily lifted and lowered by the driver using a lever alongside his seat. Unfortunately at the time the plough was launched in late 1917 Ford had started production of his own tractor, later to become the Fordson 'F', and this killed off any market there might be for this plough.

This setback did not deter Ferguson in the least and he set about designing a plough for the Fordson 'F' after he had sold his stock of original ploughs. To overcome the problem of the tractor rearing, which could happen if a trailing plough hit an obstruction, a duplex linkage consisting of two parallel links were mounted one above the other to form a semi rigid arrangement between the tractor and plough. These links were arranged so they pulled the plough down to its working depth and so enabled the weight of the plough to be kept to a minimum. It improved traction by placing the weight of the plough, and the forces involved in ploughing firmly on the tractor. One major stumbling block remained, the depth control wheel, these had not been fitted to the Eros and original Fordson ploughs, and there was still the problem of keeping the plough at an even depth.

When the plough went into production, made by the Roderick Lean Co. of Mannfield, Ohio, USA, it had to be fitted with a depth wheel. Ferguson was not happy with this and continued, assisted by his development team of Willie Sands, Archie Greer, and John Williams, to try and eliminate the depth wheel. Eventually this was achieved by having a floating skid running along the furrow bottom and connected to the duplex linkage so that as the tractor wheels crossed bumps and hollows the movement of the sid caused the plough to be raised or lowered accordingly.

In 1924, shortly after the problem had been solved the Roderick Lean Co. went bankrupt leaving Ferguson without a supplier. This did not deter him and he again set of for America. He had already made various trips there including one to demonstrate his plough to Henry Ford who offered him a job with the Ford Motor Company.

Ferguson now joined forces with the Sherman Brothers, Eber and George, and in 1925 Ferguson Sherman Inc. was formed to produce ploughs in Evansville, Indiana.

Once plough production was running smoothly, Ferguson turned his attention to improving his system by adapting it so that various other implements other than ploughs could be used. The improvements were aimed at removing the balance spring and making the tractor do the work of lifting the implement. Various ideas were tried, including an electric motor, and a mechanical system driven from the belt pulley through a pair of cone clutches, until finally a hydraulic system was devised. This was fitted onto the back of a Fordson tractor.

In 1928 Fordson production in the USA ceased and plough production also had to cease. Ferguson was back in Ireland, and did further work on the duplex linkage which was first changed to a 3 link system with single lower link and two upper links. The lower link controlled the depth and the two upper links lifted an lowered the implement; the linkage was now fitted to the tractor and not the implement.

Several companies were showing some interest in Ferguson's ideas including Allis Chalmers, Rushton, Ransomes, and the Rover Car Co. The most fruitful talks took place with the Morris Motor Co., who agreed to build a tractor using the Ferguson Hydraulic system, but at the last minute the agreement fell through. The depression of the late twenties and thirties was having an effect on much of industry at this time.

Opposite page, top, and centre. The original Ferguson plough fitted to a Ford model T with 'Eros' conversion. These two shots show the plough in and out of the ground. The plough was raised mechanically using the lever beside the driver's seat and was levelled by a lever between the rear wheels and the front of the plough.

Left: Harry Ferguson on a Fordson Model 'F'.
This tractor was used for most of the ensuing
experiments with his mounted plough.

The original plough was modified for use behind a Fordson 'F' and is seen here outside Harry Ferguson's Belfast premises.

Following further developments, the design below was reached where three point linkage was used, but there is still a depth control slipper on the plough.

Top and centre: Depth wheels were also fitted in an attempt to solve the depth control problem on some experimental ploughs. Below: Following his agreement with the Sherman Brothers, a Ferguson Sherman mechanical lift plough was marketed from 1925. The shot below shows this plough on trial behind the inevitable Fordson 'F' with the inventor watching in the left background, and it is to be noted that the design of plough follows closely resembles one used by M-F in the early 1960s. The cessation of Fordson 'F' production in the USA in 1928 also caused the plough to go out of production but work on improving it continued. The Sherman Brothers were later responsible for selling imported British Fordson 'N' models in the USA.

The black tractor built in Belfast in 1933 is seen in the three views on this page. A Hercules engine was used.

Chapter Two
The Black Tractor and the Type 'A'.

There had been talk of producing a tractor ever since the Fordson ceased production in the USA in 1928. Percival Perry, head of Ford in the United Kingdom, would not supply Fordsons direct from Cork or Dagenham to Ferguson as he felt that it was not in the interests of the Ford Motor Co. to do so.

The result was that Ferguson set about building his own tractor, which was assembled at his May Street, Belfast premises in 1933. Many components were bought in and castings in light alloy from Short's foundry were used. A Hercules engine, David Brown gearbox, and Ferguson three point linkage, resulted in a 16 cwt. machine as opposed to the 30 cwt. of the Fordson.

The Ferguson draft control which was applied to the tractor gave added adhesion when using the Ferguson implements designed specifically for the tractor. It was claimed that there need be no problem as regards the weight of the tractor, except, of course, when you towed anything behind.

Unit construction was applied and the prototype had this split into four components; engine, clutch housing, gearbox, and rear axle were flanged to each other. The clutch was a single plate unit, and a three speed constant mesh gearbox took the drive to a spiral bevel rear axle, which in design was similar to a lorry rear axle, but with the front cover flange being mated to the rear of the gearbox housing.

Independant brakes were fitted to assist turning, and the tractor was mounted on spoked type wheels similar to those on the early Fordsons. It could be operated on petrol or kerosine, but the manifold design did not allow for very efficient vaporisation of fuel oils. Ferguson preferred petrol as a tractor fuel anyway!

With a prototype, looking very much like a reduced Fordson, in existence, Ferguson then set about getting the tractor into production. David Brown of Huddersfield had supplied some components for the Black tractor and following negotiations, agreement was reached whereby David Brown Tractors Ltd., a new company, would build the tractors and Ferguson would take care of the selling.

The first type 'A' tractors were ready by May 1936, and the design of the Black tractor was followed closely. The clutch and gearbox housing were now combined, and a Coventry Climax L head engine of 3.125" bore and 4" stroke was now used. This side valve unit ran at 2000rpm and gave 20HP. It featured pressure lubrication and shell bearings which details were a distinct advantage over the Fordson engine. Unlike some units built by Climax themselves, a self starter and water pump were absent, on cost grounds. Magneto Ignition by BTH was used.

The colour of the tractor was changed to battleship grey. Ferguson wanted production models to be black but his staff persuaded him to change.

The location of the hydraulic pump however did create one nuisance in that the hydraulics would only operate when the tractor was on the move and in gear. One had to be on the move when raising the implement and this could be very awkward at headlands when ploughing.

After the first 500 tractors the Coventry Climax concern was retooling for a new engine, so David Brown bought the patterns and built the final 800 or so engines themselves.

Four implements were available initially, a 10" two furrow plough, a ridger, and spring or rigid tine cultivators. A single furrow 12" plough came later.

Allied to its own equipment the tractor performed slowly by modern standards but did the job - the engine lacked the guts needed for even two furrow ploughing. Its main shortcomings could be allied to bad manifold design which was later corrected, but not by David Brown, as several proprietory makes of Vaporisers were put on the market. Another weakness was the use of alloy castings. Some steel transmission housings were actually cast and some even fitted. This increased the weight of the tractor by about 3cwt. At least one tractor had a PTO fitted, a feature which production tractors lacked.

In the two year period of production David Brown Tractors learnt a lot about the shortcomings of the original design and tried to persuade Harry Ferguson to allow them to build a more powerful tractor; this Ferguson resisted. The two concerns parted company and David Brown started building their own VAK1 model from 1939. Although three point linkage was available on the David Brown tractor, it lacked the draft control of the Ferguson which was protected by patents.

Top: The type 'A' was often used with equipment for which it was not suitable - the horse rake shown here would however be within the capacity of the tractor.

Right: A sole prototype with cast iron transmission case and PTO was built. The PTO position is seen here - the tractor is preserved.

Below and Bottom: A Vineyard version of the type 'A' was produced and this had a set back front axle to allow for greater manoeuvrability in confined orchards and groves.

The development team are seen here posed with a model 'A' and plough. They are (left to right); John Chambers, Archie Greer, Willie Sands, and Harry Ferguson himself.

The Ferguson three point linkage was at last available on a production tractor with the introduction of the model 'A' in 1936. The whole ensemble is seen below, with the plough somewhat dwarfing the size of the tractor. With the Ferguson weight transfer system operating through the top link of the hydraulic linkage however, adhesion was no problem, bearing in mind that the tractor was built with alloy castings to keep it as light as possible.

Type 'A' ploughing with 12" plough.

Type 'A' with Bamfords mower modified for tractor operation by one man.

Type 'A' and Binder. The use of trailed equipment with the Ferguson did not allow the use of the weight transfer facility round which the tractor was designed.

A type 'A' ploughing in Yorkshire.

Above: Finished tractors come off the line at David Brown's Park Works at Huddersfield. Production was on the flow line principle, although with a total of 1200 type 'A' tractors being built, it could not be described as mass production. At the same time Fords were building around ten times the number of units in one year!

Below: Implements were also assembled at Huddersfield, this view shows ploughs and toolbars in various stages of build-up.

Opposite page: Upper; the type 'A' being demonstrated in Kent. Lower; A type 'A' fitted with belt pulley attachment driving a threshing machine.

Chapter Three
The Handshake Agreement

The demonstration of a Model 'A' tractor and plough by Harry Ferguson at Henry Ford's home - Fairlane, paved the way for the famous 'Handshake Agreement'.

The agreement provided for Ford to build the tractors and Ferguson to market them through his own selling organisation.

With the benefit of the most up to date developments in automotive engineering, the Ford design team, along with Ferguson's men Sands & Greer, created the real forerunner of the modern tractor. To speed production use of standard components was encouraged, and apart from the Ferguson Hydraulic System the tractor showed its Ford parentage very well in the use of an engine which was half a Mercury V8, and transmission and other components common with other contemporary Ford products.

Prototypes were to hand in March 1939, and by June production models were available for demonstration.

The tractor was very much in line with contemporary Ford syling, and the four cylinder side valve engine of 3.125" bore by 3.75" stroke developed 24HP at a maximum speed of 2200rpm. The engine was machined on the same line as the V8 units, an extra shift being put on to cope with the extra production.

Just how much Ferguson's team influenced the design is subject to question, as Ford design policy very much revolved round the 'team' idea, and Ferguson's three men just became - pro tem - part of that team. Certainly the hydraulic linkage was pure Ferguson, but the incorporation of the hydraulic pump into a square transmission housing and driven from the PTO seems to have originated with Sorensen. The beam type front axle was the brainchild of Sands and Greer.

The selling organisation which was set up also included the brothers Sherman, who had sold Ferguson ploughs earlier on, and the new selling Corporation was in part financed by a loan of $50,000 from Henry Ford.

The tractor was an instant success and put behind it all the weaknesses of the type 'A'.

There was, however, nothing in the agreement in the USA to allow for production of the Ford 9N in the United Kingdom. Ford of Britain were virtually independant of the parent US concern in 1939. Attempts were made to get 9N production started in the UK, but Percival Perry, head of Ford in Britain, found himself drawn into some rather unfortunate politics concerning Henry Ford.

Ford, who was recovering from the after effects of a stroke, was not in full command of the situation, and the attempts by him to force Dagenham to produce the 9N caused a rift between Perry and himself. In any case the matter was in fact outside Perry's hands, as the War in Europe had effectively placed tractor production under Government control and there was no way the Government would allow a break in production to happen.

The 9N did reach the United Kingdom; fitted with modified Holley 295 Vaporiser to run on TVO and designated the 9NAN. Ford in the UK handled all spares and service on these units imported under lease-lend.

Wartime shortages caused a utility model to be produced, on steel wheels, and without battery reliant electrics or self starter. The 2NAN was the UK equivalent of this model. Edzel Ford, Henry Ford's oldest son, who had a hand in styling the 9N, died in 1943. This left a gap in the Ford empire filled by Henry Ford II in 1945.

The new chairman had the onerous task of putting the Ford operation back into the black after the ravages of war, and his attitude to the production of a tractor sold by another organisation was hostile. Henry Ford II realised that the bad business judgement of his father had created the problem, indeed a simple agreement in writing might well have overcome many of the later unpleasantries, therefore the sales agreement was terminated in 1947. The relationship between Ferguson and Ford had sadly deteriorated, not helped by wartime shortages and the end result was that by 1948 Ford were building their own tractor, the 8N, which was simply an improved 9N, and selling it through their own sales organisation.

The new Ford tractor had a four speed rather than a three speed gearbox and improved hydraulics with means of overriding the Ferguson draft control. By this time of course the TE-20 was being built in England, a tractor of very similar design to the 8N.

The termination of the agreement naturally left a 'no supply' situation in America, and Harry Ferguson was forced to import such tractors as he could from England. He therefore filed a complaint against the Ford Motor Company on 8th January, 1948, regarding the use of the Patents held by him with regard to the hydraulic system on the Ford tractor.

The trial started on 29th March, 1951. The sum of $240,000,000 was claimed as a result of the introduction of the Ford 8N and the consequent loss in business to the Ferguson organisation, and the unlicenced use of the Ferguson system, which was patented, on the new Ford tractor.

After long and costly proceedings, Ferguson accepted a settlement of $9.250,000. This was only to cover the unauthorised use of the Ferguson hydraulic system, the claim against loss of business was dismissed.

The Ford Motor Company were instructed to stop production of the Dearborn or 8N tractor by 1952, but the Ferguson Patents had already been extended and were soon to be out of date. Ford's new 1951 model the NAA had a fully 'live' hydraulic system with engine driven hydraulic pump and its introduction necessitated the updating of the then current TO-20 model in due course. Most modern tractors now have the draft control pioneered by Harry Ferguson, usually with the Ford innovation of the over riding feature which allows the lift to be used under 'position control'. This latter feature was not approved by Ferguson, yet from the 35 on it became standard on all M-F models. In due course manufacturers such as Ford and M-F often came to reciprocal agreements over the use of each other's patents. So complex had the situation become over these that M-F and other makers set up their own patents departments run by Lawyers to ensure that any new ideas they had were covered, and also to make sure that in building anything new they were not in infingement of anybody else's patented designs.

During the war, some 2N tractors had been supplied to the US forces for airfield and other uses, without the Ferguson system, and to complete the story illustrations of these are included in this book.

Henry Ford & Harry Ferguson with the type 'A' he took to Fairlane for demonstration.

Below: The prototype 9N with rather austere styling. (Henry Ford Museum).

The final production tractor was developed in less than a year. Here Harry Ferguson and Henry Ford pose with one of the early production tractors, and a Dearborn built plough.

Above: 9Ns roll off the production line at Dearborn. This tractor is being fuelled up ready to be driven away.

Below: Some of the team involved with the development of the '9N'. They are left to right; Harry Ferguson, Henry Ford, Edsel Ford, Charles Sorensen, George B. Sherman, J. L. Williams, and Eber C. Sherman.

Above: The New York World's Fair provided the opportunity to demonstrate the 9N to the public for the first time. Here Harry Ferguson and Edsel Ford watch the president of the Fair, Mr. Grover Whalen.

Opposite Page lower, and above: At the American launch of the Ford Tractor with Ferguson System on 29th June, 1939, Henry Ford handed the tractor over to this small boy, who ably operated the tractor in the demonstration area. Another early tractor with a young operator is seen in the field below. The rowcrop capability of the 9N can be seen (right) with the wheels on this tractor set at the maximum width of 76".

Above: This shot, taken at Greenmount, Co. Antrim, Northern Ireland in October 1939 shows one of the first two tractors shipped to N. I. or indeed the U.K. It was used as a demonstrator whilst the other went to McGregor Greer of Tullylagan who backed the project financially. Note the steel rear wheels, not common until the wartime shortages produced a starter and battery-less model, the 2N.

9N tractors were turned out for use by the US forces in the War. Here are two 'militarised' versions with cabs, fenders, and lighting equipment. Around the time that these were being supplied, Edsel Ford was attempting to persuade his father to withdraw from the US tractor market altogether, as Ford Motor Co. were losing a lot of money on supplying 9N's to Ferguson. (Henry Ford Museum).

From 1942 on, the Ford 9N received a vertical bar grille, more of contemporary Ford styling. Although the two tractors shown here appear to have full electrical equipment, the 2N model was launched with no self starter, a magneto, and steel wheels in most cases instead of rubber tyres. (Henry Ford Museum).

Finished in Olive Drab, and fitted with bumpers, subframes, and grass tyres, these Ford 2N's were about to go into military service when photographed in 1943. They were supplied, less hydraulics, to the military direct, a procedure which did not help the by then somewhat strained relationship between Ford & Ferguson. (Henry Ford Museum).

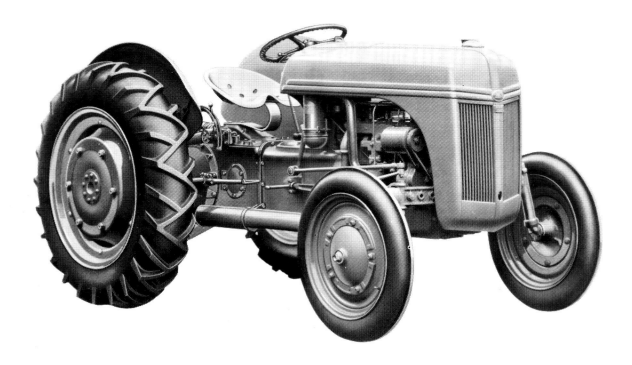

Top: The 9N after its 1942 grille restyle.

Centre: The 9NAN with Holley vaporiser was supplied under lease-lend to the United Kingdom to allow low cost TVO fuel to be used.

Right: 9N tractors lined up for a demonstration.

Although equipped for the benefit of mounted implements, this wartime shot of a Ford 9NAN in England shows the Rowcrop facility to advantage, but the use of a somewhat outdated horse drill renders the Ferguson System redundant in this case.

The Ford 8N was Ford's answer to the break with Ferguson. It featured an extra forward speed, improved hydraulics, and other detail differences. Fords built and sold some 442000 of these tractors from 1947 - 1952.

Chapter Four
The TE-20

Ask any Ford salesman of the late forties and early fifties what he feared most and he would tell you "The Grey Menace". Such was the success of the product of a new relationship between Harry Ferguson and the Standard Motor Co. which provided the Irishman with a tractor which, for the first time, challenged the supremacy of Ford in the United Kingdom.

Following the failure of getting 9N production started in the UK, and the breakdown of the 'Handshake Agreement' in the USA, Harry Ferguson was left without a tractor to sell in the United Kingdom. It was fortunate that a surplus capacity in the automotive industry was evident by 1945; having ceased military work many of the motor manufacturers were looking for ways to use the 'shadow factories' of the war years.

Such a plant existed at Banner Lane in Coventry and, approached by Harry Ferguson, Sir John Black of the Standard Motor Company was receptive of the idea of building tractors there, indeed it was hoped that the whole range of Ferguson Implements could also be produced. With continued Government restrictions, there would be problems in obtaining the correct tooling and materials.

At the time Standard were about to develop a new engine for the new postwar family saloon car - which became the Vanguard on its appearance in July 1947. This could be adapted to fit the tractor, but in order to get production started engines had to be obtained from elsewhere.

There was a great need in postwar years to earn dollars and as the new tractor would primarily be for Eastern Hemisphere sale this created difficulties with the Ministry of Supply. Licences had to be obtained to import anything and permits had to be obtained to allow purchase of any materials, from a washer to a complete machine tool.

An approach to Sir Stafford Cripps, Chancellor of the Exchequer in Britain's new Labour Government, was made by Harry Ferguson, and suitably impressed at the possibility of bringing work to war torn Coventry, arranged sanctions for machine tools and raw materials. There was a twist to this however, as the permit for engine imports was only to last until as long as it took to get the new engine into production at Coventry. Now by getting the funds to develop a new engine, ostensibly for the tractor, the same engine was also to be used in the new car. Some clever bargaining by Sir John Black with the Ministry of Transport ensured that the engine was sanctioned and it was phased into tractor production in 1948. As the new car was a potential dollar earner, and 60% of production was to be for export, the first engines actually went into the cars, their export in effect countering the import of the 'Continental Z-120' engines. Early advertising for the Vanguard car even played on the fact that alternative engines were being economically produced for both cars and tractors.

As for the tractor itself, it was simply an updated 9N with four speed gearbox, and the benefit of an overhead valve engine.

While problems in the Western Hemisphere were involving Harry Ferguson, production at Banner Lane built up satisfactorily, and in due course the tractors became 100% Standard engined.

There was of course one disadvantage with the Ferguson System, and that one required the proper implements to use with the tractor for it to reach its full potential. Unfortunately the idea of these being built at Coventry soon evaporated, and it was from a multitude of engineering firms and machinery suppliers that the tools for the three point linkage came. At least with the other makes of tractor which were designed for trailed implements some adaptation of horse drawn tackle could be made as a stopgap, but not with the Ferguson. Its weight distribution did not make it suitable for hauling certain types of implement.

The second problem was that the tractor ran on Petrol. Now, in theory, petrol was still rationed in 1946; indeed it was 1950 before all restrictions on its use were lifted. Enough fuel could be obtained in the usual way for agricultural use, but it was subject to excise duty, whereas TVO was not.

Harry Ferguson was initially against a low cost fuel variant, but as the home market gradually opened up it became necessary to add the TED-20 to the range. This required an engine with a lower compression ratio and suitable vaporiser. Indeed once the TVO model had been established, a zero octane (lamp oil) model was also offered for export from 1950.

The Petrol engine developed 28.4hp at the belt and was of 80mm bore and 92mm stroke. Now the car version of the engine was, after initial development, set at 85mm. Again Ferguson was not keen to increase the power output of the tractor. He was want to point out that it defeated the object of the exercise.

The problem arose that the TVO model was only rated at 26hp at the belt, and it was pointed out that by using the larger bore engine the power could be increased to that of the petrol version. This was agreed, but when the change to the 85mm engine took place on 22nd January, 1951, at serial 172501, the larger engine was fitted to all spark ignition models.

With the competition fitting diesels in production, it was not long before Ferguson's sales force were calling for a diesel version of the TE-20. Now as Harry Ferguson himself was not a diesel fan, it took some considerable persuasion to get him to agree to a diesel engined tractor at all.

Although the source of the Petrol and TVO engines for the TE-20 tractors built in the Eastern Hemisphere was of course the same Standard Motor Company, Ferguson was under no obligation to buy engines from that concern. At the time of development the only really suitable engine available was the Perkins P3, and this was still under development.

Perkins offered the P4, but but it was a rather expensive item, (as was the P3), and developed too much power in the eyes of Harry Ferguson. Freeman Sanders became involved in the design work on the diesel engine which was commissioned initially by Ferguson. Part of the deal was that development costs would be shared equally if the same engine could be adapted for use in the Vanguard car. In the end H.F. had to bear all the development costs, as by the time the car went diesel, Massey Harris had become involved on the tractor side.

The resultant unit was dry linered, and had a bore and stroke of 3-3/16" x 4", indirect injection layout, chain driven camshaft and fuel injection pump, and turned out some 2Cwt heavier and 1.25" longer than the petrol unit. This meant that it was not conceivable to provide units to convert previous production tractors to diesel, as the build of the TEF-20 as it was designated on its introduction in June 1951 had to take dimensional variations into account. Kigass equipment was provided to aid starting, but even with this feature the engine had a reputation for sluggish starting in cold weather. A single heater plug was situated in the inlet manifold. Strange to say, when the engine was finally fitted in the Vanguard car in 1955 separate heater plugs for each cylinder were provided - some engines of this type did eventually get into a few tractors.

The only effect that this had on other models was the adaptation of 12 volt electrics for all models from the 250001st tractor in 1952. This was in any case only following the trend in general for 12 volt systems in the whole motor industry.

In addition to the standard tractor, demand grew for narrower versions once the potential of use in vineyards and orchards was realised. The factory built narrow version came out in 1946. This lost 6" in width by fitment of narrower axle shafts. In 1952 the Vineyard model became a factory assembled option and by the use of smaller tyres a reduction in overall height of 2" was achieved in addition to a reduced width of 32" minimum track.

The diesel model was never offered in Narrow or Vineyard form in TE-20 days, although conversions were offered by Reekie Engineering, Jack Oldings, etc. These firms had started by converting standard spark ignition tractors, indeed some Ford/Ferguson 9Ns were also dealt with.

By the early fifties tractors were also becoming more used in industry, and a whole range of allied equipment was advertised for use with the Ferguson, from mobile compressors to a complete drive on roller. A pleathora of variations were offered for industrial use, from basic tractors to those with full front and rear fenders, extra braking, and lighting, to comply with the Road Traffic Acts.

Everybody thought that the TE-20 would go on for ever, but already, as we have seen, the model had been effectively superseded in the Western Hemisphere. Over half a million Grey Fergies were built from 1946-56, at the time the largest production run of any tractor in the UK.

The Ferguson TE-20 closely resembled the Ford Ferguson 9N. Easy identification of tractors assembled in the U.K. with Continental engines can be made by noting the kink in the exhaust after it leaves the manifold.

The TE-20 with British built Ferguson plough.

Below: The TE-20 with its weight transfer system did not really need the addition of steel wheel equipment for adhesion except in the most arduous conditions.

Above: The Continental Engined TE-20. Unlike the Ford 9N which had a service flap to gain access to fuel caps, the whole bonnet on the TE-20 tilted forward.

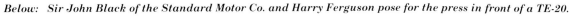

Below: Sir John Black of the Standard Motor Co. and Harry Ferguson pose for the press in front of a TE-20.

Harry Ferguson's publicity stunts often smacked of the bizarre. he staged his postwar press conference at Claridges' to launch the TE-20 onto world markets, and proceeded to drive it across the ballroom, and then to the consternation of hotel staff, through the crowded lobby and out into the street. The tractor is an early TEA-20 with Standard 80mm engine. Careful preparation ensured that the tractor was 'dry' - there was no oil in the sump in case of leakage, and only a cupful of petrol was put in the tank. Even so, the engine was dismantled later in the experimental dept. at Fletchampstead, Coventry, and no ill effects were found.

Above: Harry Ferguson at home at Abbotswood, near Lower Swell, Gloucestershire, where he lived from 1946. He is holding the American papers giving news of his legal suit with Ford Motor Company.

Below: Ferguson is seen with legal advisers prior to his court case against Ford proceeding.

Above and Below: The TEA-20 with Standard engine - similar to that fitted to the Standard Vanguard car had a successful 8 year run. Various modifications were made over that period. The engine was bored out to 85mm from 22nd January 1951, and 12 volt electrics were fitted from tractor 200,001.

The TED-20 (V.O.) and TEH-20 (lamp oil) models were introduced from 1949, and can be easily identified by the manifold shield.

Above: The Ferguson TED-20 was the most popular model with UK farmers until the diesel engine was developed.   The inevitable problems occurred when the tractor was used on light work when running on TVO however.

Below: Tractor 200000 comes off the line at Banner Lane.   This was in theory the last of the 6 volt tractors; however it would appear that some were built later.   Harry Ferguson and Sir John Black are again prominent.

The narrow version of the TE 20 catered for situations where it proved impossible to use a normal width tractor. A TEC-20 (petrol) model is seen here, whilst TEE-20 (V.O.) and TEJ-20 (Lamp oil) models were also available, the latter being introduced in April 1950. Track width was 42" instead of the 48" of the standard model.

Introduced in April 1952, the Vineyard model closed a gap in the sales area which had been covered by dealers doing their own conversions. A TEL-20 (V.O.) model is seen here with wheels set at the normal track of 32". The same model is seen below with track set out to the width of a normal tractor.

Above: A comparison of the rear of the Vineyard model with track set fully out, and at the normal 32" setting.

Below: The reduced height of the Vineyard model is seen when compared with a normal width tractor.

A vineyard tractor at work.

Above and below: The Diesel engined TEF-20. The engine was longer and could not be fitted to existing Ferguson tractors. The clutch housing was also different as the starter was on the RH. side of the engine. Note the location of the batteries and the chief identification feature, the pre cleaner below the exhaust manifold.

Right: The diesel engine installation. The unit was developed in conjunction with Freeman Sanders.

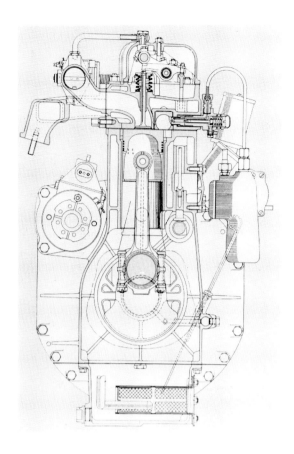

Above: The right side of the diesel engine installation. A considerable number of these tractors are still at work in 1990!

Right: The diesel engine in section showing the patented pre-combustion chamber, making it an indirect injection unit.

Below: Tractor 500000 has been preserved at the Ferguson Museum at Banner Lane, and is seen here at work in more recent times, with one of its successors, the 135, in the background.

The basic industrial tractor TEP-ZD, a petrol model with Agricultural mudguards.

A similar model with diesel engine designated TET-ZD.

A semi-industrial model was also available, this is a TET-20T Diesel model.

Above: The full industrial model featured dual brakes (hydro mechanical), fenders, bumper, grille guard and industrial tyres. Full Ferguson hydraulics were fitted and a range of approved implements and industrial equipment was available, made by outside manufacturers.   The lighting equipment was designed to comply with the Road Traffic Acts.

The Last TE-20 comes off the line in 1956.   This was serial number 517651, and completed the run of over half a million units in just under ten years.

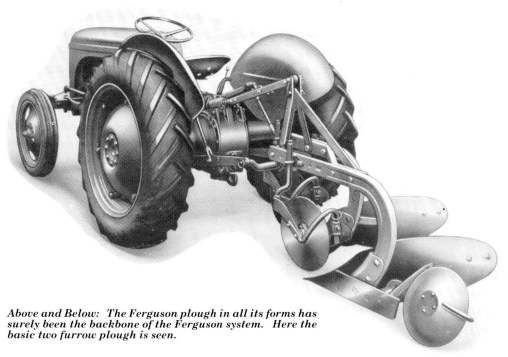

Above and Below: The Ferguson plough in all its forms has surely been the backbone of the Ferguson system. Here the basic two furrow plough is seen.

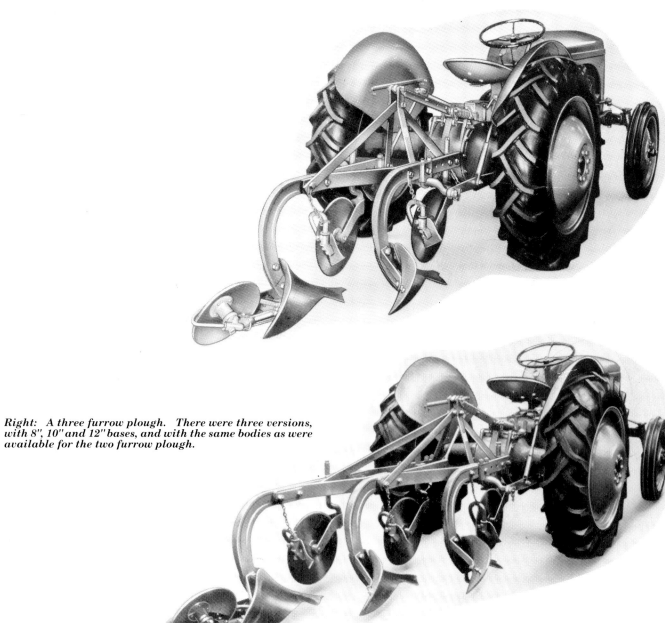

Right: A three furrow plough. There were three versions, with 8", 10" and 12" bases, and with the same bodies as were available for the two furrow plough.

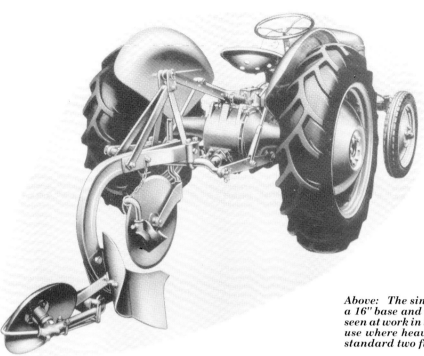

Above: The single furrow plough. This was designed with a 16" base and deep digger body. The same plough can be seen at work in the bottom illustration, and was intended for use where heavy conditions would not allow the use of the standard two furrow unit.

Below: The two furrow plough was available with 10" or 12" bases and with general purpose or semi digger bodies. The 10" plough could be converted into a 3 furrow unit using a conversion kit.

Above and Right: The reversible plough, model T-AE-28, was a single furrow plough with a 16" base and deep digger body. The plough was automatically tripped. During work the body not in use helped to add weight to the tractor land wheel. Note the wheel girdles on the tractor.

Left and Below: The single furrow reversible plough at work.

The disc plough models 2-P-AE-20 (2 furrow) and 3-P-AE-20 (3 furrow) were rarely seen in the UK.

This implement has proved so popular in the Middle East that it has stayed in production as the 769 Disc Plough until the present day.

The two furrow plough fitted with quick adjustment lever.

Right: Model 95-ME-20 Spring tine cultivator, for light general use. The tines could be rearranged on the toolbar for rowcrop use.

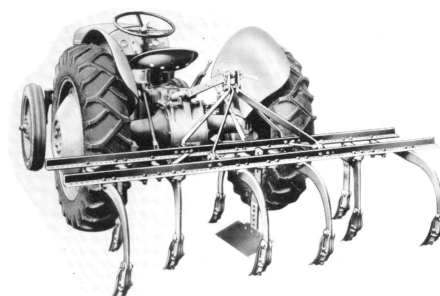

Right: This model rigid tine was for heavier use than the machine above.

Below: This machine gives a good shatter effect in heavy land and can be safely used on stoney ground with less chance of damage due to the spring tines.

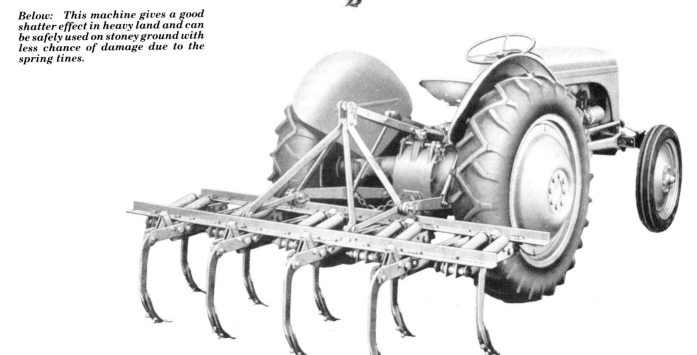

Left: The spring tine cultivator at work.

The steerage hoe at work.   This is the model IB-ME-20 without discs.

Below: Harry Ferguson using the tiller at his home at Abbotswood.

Below: The model B-ME-20 4 row steerage hoe (with discs) was developed for precision rowcrop cultivation and was steered by the tiller acting on a rod connecting the implement to one of the tractor lower links.

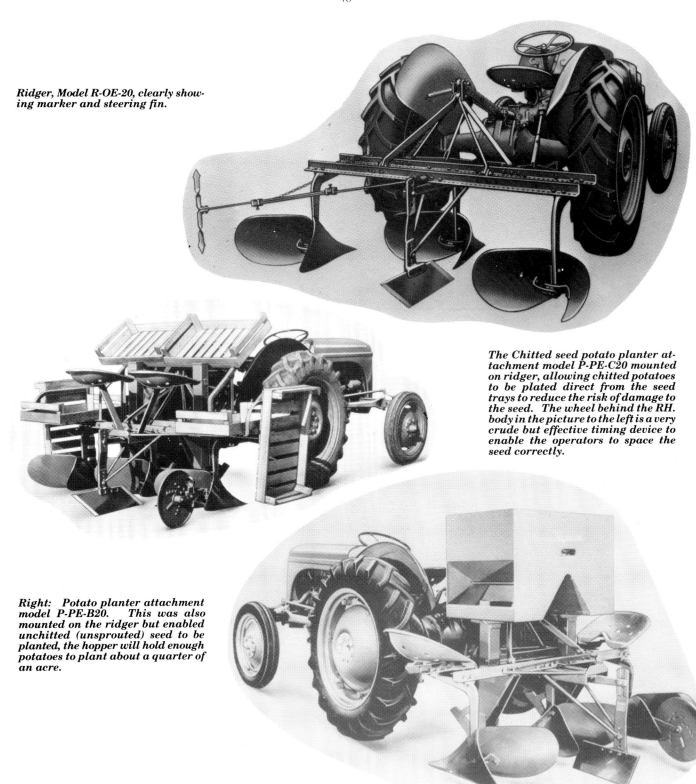

Ridger, Model R-OE-20, clearly showing marker and steering fin.

The Chitted seed potato planter attachment model P-PE-C20 mounted on ridger, allowing chitted potatoes to be plated direct from the seed trays to reduce the risk of damage to the seed. The wheel behind the RH. body in the picture to the left is a very crude but effective timing device to enable the operators to space the seed correctly.

Right: Potato planter attachment model P-PE-B20. This was also mounted on the ridger but enabled unchitted (unsprouted) seed to be planted, the hopper will hold enough potatoes to plant about a quarter of an acre.

The whole ensemble lifted clear of the ground by the TE-20's hydraulic three point linkage.

The planter in action, the ridged portion of the field to the left having been planted and the final section to the right is as yet unseeded.

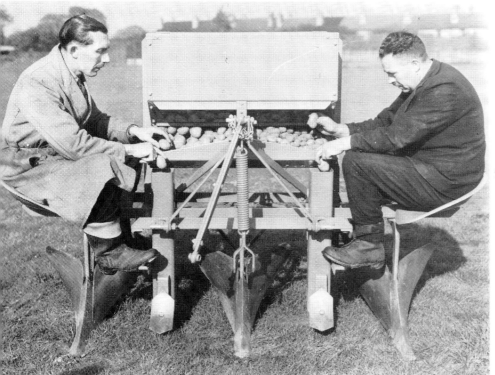

The posed shot shows the operators dropping seeds into the chutes.

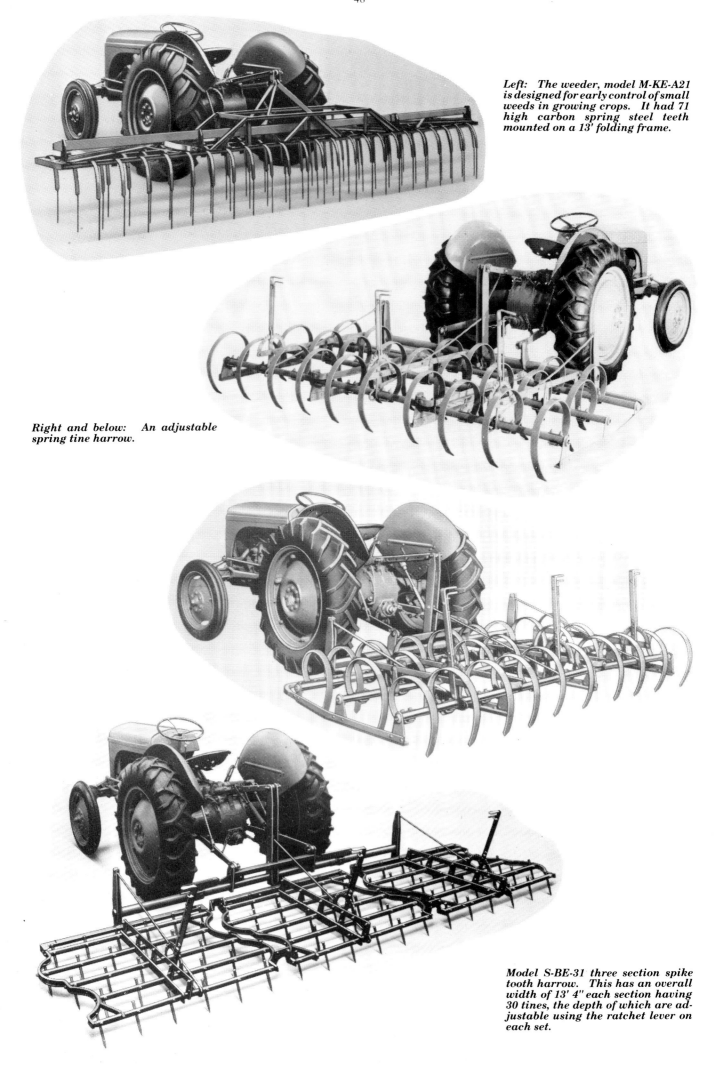

Left: The weeder, model M-KE-A21 is designed for early control of small weeds in growing crops. It had 71 high carbon spring steel teeth mounted on a 13' folding frame.

Right and below: An adjustable spring tine harrow.

Model S-BE-31 three section spike tooth harrow. This has an overall width of 13' 4" each section having 30 tines, the depth of which are adjustable using the ratchet lever on each set.

Above: Whilst in the 1990s an increasing problem is the width of implements and continual work is in hand to enable easy transportation along public roads, in the late forties this problem was also true of some of the implements used with the Ferguson. The implement is seen here in the transport position.

Right: The weeder in operation.

Left: The weeder being folded for transit.   It was a lightweight machine and due to this a balance spring is fitted between the tractor and implement to ensure accurate draft control.   Although these machines went out of fashion with the increasing use of chemical sprays and pesticides, they are again coming into use as organic farming grows in popularity.   The pictures on this page were taken behind the Fletchampstead Highway/ Tile Hill Lane headquarters of Harry Ferguson Ltd.   This is now headquarters of the Austin-Rover Group.

Above: The mounted disc harrow, models 4A-BE-22 (7' width) and 2A-BE-22 (6' width) was one of the most important implements in confirming the 'Ferguson System' in the forefront of world agriculture, giving the ability to use a small tractor with an implement previously only being capable of being pulled by a larger and heavier tractor

Above: The previous design of disc harrow was less compact and were coupled to the tractor three point linkage but could not be transported on same.

Below: The offset disc harrow model G-BE-20 had a maximum working width of 7'3" and was designed for use in vineyards and orchards where it could reach under overhanging branches. It could also be used for field discing in heavy soil.

Above: The offset disc harrow at work in an orchard.

Right, below, and bottom: Three models of reversible heavy duty disc harrows were produced. IH-BE-20 of 5' 6" cut with 8 - 22" discs, 3H-BE-20 of 7' cut with 10 - 22" discs, and 5E-BE-20 of 5' 6" cut with 8 - 23" discs. They were often used in hot climates to produce terraces for conserving winter moisture thus enabling crops to be grown in the summer heat.

Above: **The grain drill, model G-PE-A20 was later redesignated a 'Multi purpose seed drill.' It was a 13 row, ground driven implement with a hopper capacity of 6 bushels.**

Right: **The potato spinner model D-HE-20**

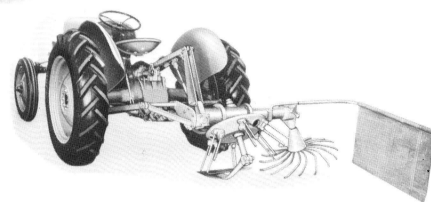

Left: **The spinner broadcaster, model FF-30 was a machine which did not take on. A sound design, it was perhaps the fact that artificial fertilizers had not really taken off in the early fifties.**

Below: **The low volume sprayer, model G-LE-20 was another case of 'Badge Engineering', and was produced by Fisons Pest Control. In a pre-plastics era, this type of sprayer suffered from the basic fault of a metal tank which tended to corrode fairly rapidly.**

Above: The drill was designed and built by Lundells. It is seen here at work sowing weed corn, and (right) being filled.

Below: Here the drill is in use as a fertiliser distributor with the Fertiliser attachment fitted which effectively produced a combined fertiliser and grain drill.

Right: The potato spinner is an implements which a considerable number of farms still have tucked away, to be dragged out and put to use to open up headlands or in a wet year when more modern harvesters are floundering in the mud.

Above and Left: The subsoiler, model D-BE-28 was designed for breaking up the subsoil and plough pans, and would work to a depth of 18" - for use in grassland a disc coulter was available.

The grader blade was also useful for clearing slurry from concrete yards with the onslaught of the milking parlour.

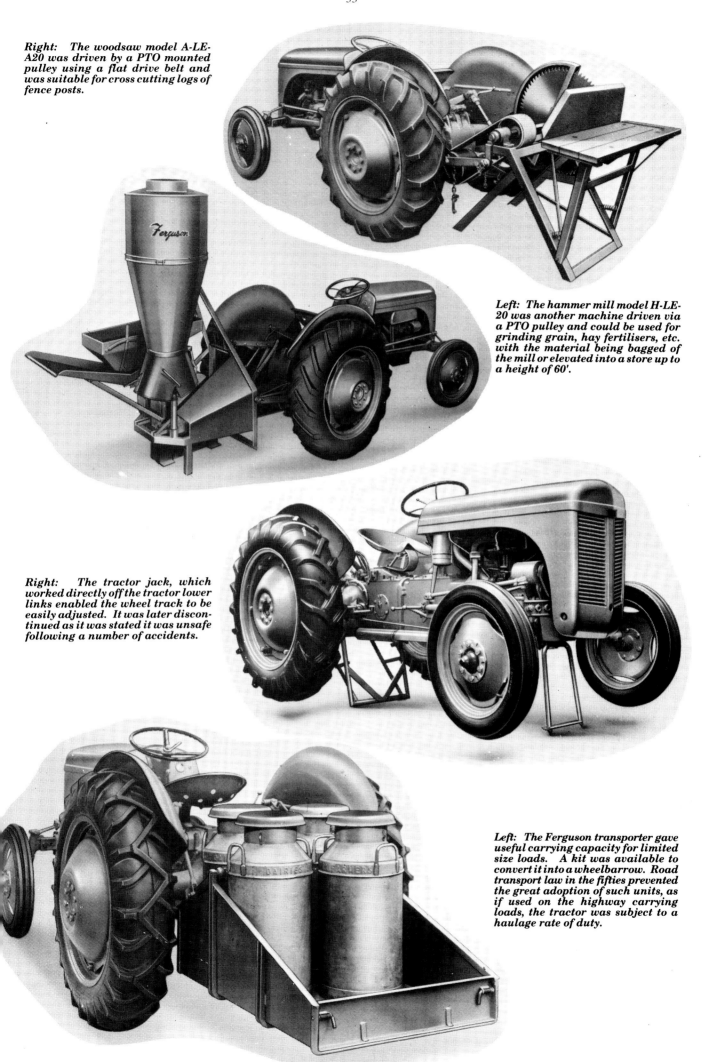

Right: The woodsaw model A-LE-A20 was driven by a PTO mounted pulley using a flat drive belt and was suitable for cross cutting logs of fence posts.

Left: The hammer mill model H-LE-20 was another machine driven via a PTO pulley and could be used for grinding grain, hay fertilisers, etc. with the material being bagged of the mill or elevated into a store up to a height of 60'.

Right: The tractor jack, which worked directly off the tractor lower links enabled the wheel track to be easily adjusted. It was later discontinued as it was stated it was unsafe following a number of accidents.

Left: The Ferguson transporter gave useful carrying capacity for limited size loads. A kit was available to convert it into a wheelbarrow. Road transport law in the fifties prevented the great adoption of such units, as if used on the highway carrying loads, the tractor was subject to a haulage rate of duty.

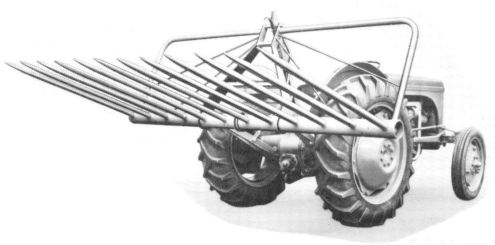

The illustrations on this page all show the model G-EE-20 buckrake. A 12 tine implement with an overall width of 8' 8" and a carrying capacity of 750 lbs. The design of the top link allowed the buckrake to follow the ground contour without digging in. A 10 tine model - A10-SEE was also available with an overall width of 7' 2". When using these implements it was advised to fit front wheel weights to the tractor.

Above and Left: The model U-UE-20 'Hesford Patent Linkage Winch for the Ferguson System'. This winch was manufactured by C. M. Hesford Ltd., of Ormskirk, Lancs., and weighed 6 cwt. with a rated pull of 7000 lbs. 40 feet of wire rope was supplied with a breaking strain of 11760 lbs., (5.25 tons), and alternative rope lengths of 60, 80 or 100 feet were available as an option.

Above and left: The post hole digger model 90/120-FE-20 had a choice of 9" or 12" augers and could dig a hole 3' deep in most soil conditions. An 18" diameter auger was introduced at a later date.

Above: The Ferguson 3 ton trailer was one of the first trailers to offer a degree of weight transfer with one third of the load carried by the tractor.

Right: The prototype TEF-20 diesel seen with the 3 ton trailer outside the old blacksmith's cottage at Langley in Warwickshire. The driver is Mr T. Sherwen, who at the time was involved in the design and development of Ferguson equipment.

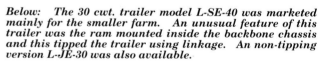

Below: The 30 cwt. trailer model L-SE-40 was marketed mainly for the smaller farm. An unusual feature of this trailer was the ram mounted inside the backbone chassis and this tipped the trailer using linkage. An non-tipping version L-JE-30 was also available.

Above: This farmyard scene shows the original design of the 3 ton trailer.   It was designed in Detroit, and built in the UK by GKN. After around 3500 were built it became evident that the original design, which involved the tractor's three point linkage being attached directly to the trailer, proved difficult to operate; it was often impossible to latch the lower link if ground conditions were slippery. A kit was later introduced to fit the trailer with a normal drawbar, and the problems caused the urgency for the development of a pick-up hitch.

Below: This TE-20 and loaded 30cwt. trailer are seen leaving Park Farm, Stareton, just along the road from the Royal Showground at Stoneleigh in Warwickshire and not far from the M-F training school and complex.

The lightweight loader. Model L-UE-20 was designed for use with the manure spreader or with the 30 cwt. trailer. it was not suitable for higher trailers as it had a maximum height of 66" and a tripped clearance at the fork tines of 48". the loader had a maximum tearaway capacity of 1000 lbs. and a nominal load of 600 lbs.

Below: A concrete weight was available for attachment.

At work in the muck. We regret that we are unable to supply the 'smell' on these pages, but readers can no doubt imagine it.

The mounting of the loader on the front axle reduced effective handling space and the width in which the unit could operate.

Loading the muck spreader.

All loaded up and ready to go. This ensemble took the hard work out of muck handling.

Left: Originally called the cantilever loader, this machine was actually the high lift loader, model M-UE-20, although it became known to farmers as the banana loader. It had a discharge height of 11' and a gross lifting capacity of 10 cwts. An hydraulic push-off action manure fork was available as well as a gravel bucket. The provision of a hydraulic service at the working end of the loader was the first farm loader to have this feature.

Below: The manure spreader, model A-JE-A20. This was for use with the foregoing loaders and when used with the Ferguson pick-up hitch it was possible to load and spread up to 25 loads a day.   The bottom shot shows it being loaded ready for use.

Above: The spreader would carry up to 35 cwt., although loads of about 25 cwt. were more common, and the spreading base was variable from 4 to 20 loads (6 to 30 tons) per acre.

Left: The loader fitted to an industrial TE-20 with gravel bucket. This loader was one of the first to offer hydraulic control of the bucket.

The earth scoop was intended for industrial users, but found agricultural use as well.

The rear mounted mower was available in 2 sizes, the model 5A-EE-B20 (5' cut) and the model 6A-EE-B20 (6' cut). The 6' machine was produced mainly for export. The scene of the mower at work in the lower illustration evokes happy memories - the smell of the newly cut grass, and the tractor exhaust - that is assuming that it is a TED-20 TVO model!

Above: The side delivery rake model D-EE-20 was designed primarily for use after 7' mowers in overseas conditions, although it was also successfully used in the UK with cutter bars down to 5' width.

With the advent of Combine Harvesters the baler came into its own and here a Massey Harris 701 baler is towed round by a TED-20. The engine on the baler was an Armstrong Siddeley 2 cylinder diesel and with independent power to run the baler it would bale! With the merger of Ferguson and Massey Harris some later 700 series balers had the Standard Motor Co. 85mm petrol engine fitted.

Top: A Ferguson tractor being demonstrated at Chartwell to Winston Churchill. Also in the picture are Anthony Eden and Christopher Soames.

Centre and Right: Harry Ferguson using one of his tractors at Abbotswood.

Ferguson tractors were also used with conventional implements and these three views show the harvest being cut by various reapers handled by TE-20 tractors.

A reaper at work in Northamptonshire.

Ferguson tractors were to be found at work around the world. Above: This Ferguson TE-20 replaced 7 horses on a 7-man co-operative farm in Denmark.

Left: Complete with cage wheels, this tractor is disc harrowing in a swamp in the East Indies.

Below: Timber hauling in Sweden with the aid of half tracks.

Opposite page. Top: A Ferguson is delivered to the Vatican for use on the farms controlled by the Church of Rome. Centre: Amongst bananas, this TEF-20 is seen discing. Bottom: Handling a 'Big log' in Norway with a TE-20.

The weight transfer system is seen being put to good use here in clearing afforested areas in Norway.

Road sweeping in Denmark.

A NATO base near Copenhagen finds this TEA-20 hauling a jet fighter.

This classic shot shows a Ferguson TEF-20 bringing in the sheaves to be threshed at this Perthshire farm.

Steel wheels. Strangely no road bands were offered for these.

Skeleton steel wheels. These replaced the normal wheel rim.

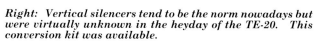

Above: Lighting kit with additional side lamps.

Right: Vertical silencers tend to be the norm nowadays but were virtually unknown in the heyday of the TE-20. This conversion kit was available.

Accessories

Left: A tip up seat and footboards were popular accessories. American built tractors had these features as standard, whilst safety regulations caused the fitting of these, and fan guards to many TE-20s in the late 'fifties.

Below: The tachometer kit.

Above left: Dual rear wheels were available.

Above right: A PTO conversion kit to allow the use of non standard shafts.

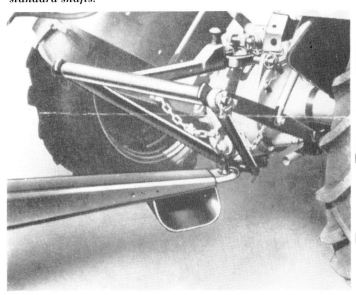

Above: The pick-up hitch. This was developed for use with the Ferguson trailers, and eliminated all the previous hitching problems.

Above Right: A stabiliser kit was available for use with the TE-20 three point linkage.

Right and Below Right: The pulley attachment could be used either side of the PTO housing.

Below: The tractor cover.

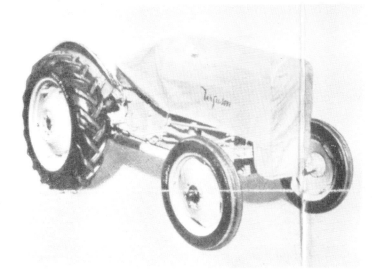

Chapter Five
Developments in the USA

The end of the relationship between Henry Ford and Harry Ferguson almost put paid to the US market as far as Ferguson was concerned. The production capacity of Ford, now that they had ceased to supply Ferguson, and launched the new 8N Dearborn tractor complete with its range of implements, would build some 442000 plus units from 1947-52. This tractor was based on the 9N but had an extra speed, and improved hydraulics, and was built from July 1947.

In the meantime, Ferguson had acquired a small plant near Detroit, and in October 1948 production of the TO-20 (tractor overseas) was started. This was very similar to the TE-20 and used the same Continental Z-120 engine. Naturally sub-assemblies and electrical components came from U.S. suppliers. A number of TE-20 tractors were imported from 1947, and this is one of the reasons why, sdespite the Standard engine being used in U.K. production from 1947, tractors built at Coventry used the Continental Z-120 engine until July 1948. Some 60000 TO-20 tractors were built up to August 1951. In the same period Ford built and sold 7 times the number of 8N tractors!

The tractor market in the USA postwar was far more competitive

than that in the UK in postwar years. Although the Lawsuit with Ford's had the effect of causing the production of the 8N to be stopped, Ford's were ready for this and launched a new model in late 1952, the NAA. Ferguson was ready for this in the USA, and launched the TO-30 from August 1951. This used the larger Continental Z-129 engine which had a 3.25" bore and 3.875" stroke. Hydraulics were improved The "Scotch Yoke Piston" type pump worked at up to 2300 psi. on all US built Ferguson TO-20s and 30s. Continental remained the main source for engines in the Detroit built tractors until the diesel and Perkins took over in the late fifties.

In 1954 the TO-35 was introduced. The Z134 Continental engine now had a bore stretched to 3 5/16". Like all U.S. built Ferguson tractors to date it retained six volt electrics, but had a redesigned gearbox with six forward speeds, and an improved four piston hydraulic pump. Position control was introduced to the hydraulics; this was done as Ford models from 1948 had been thus equipped, and despite this facility effectively 'locking out' the Ferguson draft control by now HF was only a part of the Massey Harris Ferguson concern, and market demands, in the Western Hemisphere at least, held sway. The TO-35 retained the TO-20 appearance, but was finished in a green and grey colour scheme in deference to the then Ford colours of red and grey. A diesel version, using imported Standard 23C engines, was also offered.

Following the M-H-F merger a 'two-line' policy of tractor sales was pursued and in response to the requirements of the Ferguson dealerships for a rowcrop tractor the Ferguson 40 was introduced in

1956. This was in fact a 'cosmetic job', as the model started life as the Massey Harris 50 to give M-H dealers a Ferguson system tractor with all crop capability. The then current range of M-H tractors was not enjoying customer confidence. The M-H 50 and the Ferguson 40 were mechanically identical with the TO-35 save for the provision of a conventional beam type front axle and forecarriage which could be changed for a single front, or vee twin wheels. This required the use of a single steering arm. The air cleaner was fitted in front of the radiator and provision was made for power steering.

The Ferguson 40 was sold for only two years, and was finished in a beige/green colour scheme, as were all tractors sold through former Ferguson dealerships from 1957.

From 1958 the two line policy was phased out and the two models were abandoned in favour of a revised Massey Ferguson 50 finished in red and metallic grey, but with styling more in keeping with the Massey-Harris precursor. In addition the Perkins 3 cylinder 3A-152 diesel was fitted into this machine. The Massey Ferguson 65 Dieselmatic introduced at the same time in the USA used the Perkins 4 cylinder 4A-203 engine, and had almost identical styling. From 1960 the 65 diesel sold in the USA became identical with its Eastern Hemisphere counterpart, and in due course this received the improved, direct injection Perkins AD4.203 engine. The MF35 diesel also adopted the Perkins 3A-152 engine.

In addition to normal models the M-H-F 202 and Massey Ferguson 202 and 204 were offered in the USA. These models were for industrial and commercial use and featured optional power steering. The 204 had a 'Reverse-O-Matic' transmission consisting of a flywheel mounted torque convertor, plus hydraulically activated forward and reverse multiple disc clutches, giving pedal operated instant forward and reverse.

The end of the two line policy in the USA also meant the virtual end of the Massey Harris lineage as far as tractors were concerned. Armed with the new Perkins engine facility at Peterborough the trend was towards diesel power in all models.

The first new model to appear was the MF 85 in 1959. This was available with a Continental 242 cu. in. gasoline engine, the same engine adapted to run on LPG, or a Continental 276.5 cu. in. diesel. This model was renamed the 88 in 1960. In 1961 the Super 90 Diesel replaced the 88, and this had either Continental Gasoline/LPG engines or a Perkins A4.300 diesel. This latter engine was the first specifically built at Peterborough for tractor use, and all mountings were cast into the cylinder block, rather than being bolted on. The A4.300 had a bore and stroke of 4.5 x 4.75" and developed 61/68HP @ 2000rpm. The Super 90 was built until 1965.

One final line of development needs to be looked at before closing this chapter. Massey Harris had a presence in France where 'Pony' tractors had been assembled from early postwar years. It was the French plant which was chosen to build the MF25; called a replacement for the TE-20 in some quarters. This tractor had a Perkins 4.107 diesel of 3.125" bore and 3.5" stroke which gave 20/24HP @ 2000rpm.

This model was imported into the USA, but not into the UK. The prototype of this model was in fact a Fergie 20 fitted with a Perkins 4.99 engine; the 4.107 being a bored out version of the latter.

Above and left: Harry Ferguson speaking to the workforce on the occasion of the first TO-20 coming off the line at Detroit in 1948. The tractor used the same Continental Z-120 engine as was used in the UK, but note the other design differences such as the Delco Remy electrics and the footboards.

Top: TO-20s come off the line at the Detriot plant.

Centre: The TO-30 featured a larger engine. Here one of the first tractors comes off the line; note the badge on the bonnet which identifies this model.

Right: A TO-30 at work with a grader blade.

Left: The TO-35 retained '20' styling but in other respects it was almost identical to the British built model which took another two years to appear.

The Ferguson 40 was a 'Fergieised' Massey Harris 50 and only differed in sheet metalwork design. The tractors are seen being loaded at Ferguson's Detroit plant below.

The Ferguson 40 was introduced as an All Crop version of the TO-35. It can be seen here on the left with single front wheel, below with vee twin front wheels.

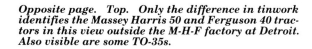

Below: A high clearance version was also available with wide front axle. Such a tractor is seen at work. Note the 'Power Shift' rear wheels.

Opposite page. Top. Only the difference in tinwork identifies the Massey Harris 50 and Ferguson 40 tractors in this view outside the M-H-F factory at Detroit. Also visible are some TO-35s.

Centre and bottom: The MF 35 as sold in the USA adopted red and metallic grey colours from 1959 and was available with the Perkins diesel from 1959. We see here a Deluxe specification tractor at work and at rest. with 'Power Shift' rear wheels, extra fuel capacity. and oversize tyres.

Chapter Six
The Massey Harris Connection

Massey Harris had been building their own tractors in Canada and the USA since 1917. In 1928 they bought out the J. I. Case Plow Works, who built tractors under the Wallis name.

From 1931 the first true M-H tractors, the 20-30 and 15-22 were launched, the smaller model forming the basis of the 'Pacemaker' and 'Challenger' models of the later thirties. Just prewar, a new range of models, the 80, 100 and 200 series arrived in 1939-39. There were revisions postwar to create the 20, 30, 40 and 50 series, which continued through the merger to become the 300, 400 and 500 series. Only a few Massey Harris tractors were sold in the United Kingdom in prewar days; a number came in under lease lend during the war, and the M-H name was best known for implements.

In 1947, the Ground Nut scheme was responsible for M-H building tractors in the USA, and imported 44 frames were initially fitted with Perkins P6 (TA) engines at Manchester. After only 16 were built production was transferred to Kilmarnock, in 1949. Whilst the intention was to export most 744s, the model failed miserably on the UK market and in 1952 only 68 were sold vis a vis 5225 exported.

In 1953 tractors built numbered 2546 and the 744 was discontinued. It was replaced by the 745 with the Perkins L4 (TA) engine, and improved hydraulic lift, and continued in production, albeit spasmodically, until 1958. Towards the end of production the supply of cast frames dried up, and to try and cut costs the 745S was introduced which had channel side frames. The M-F 65 effectively replaced the 745, and as the Transatlantic market had had the M-H 50 for some time, the Massey Harris line of tractors both in Eastern and Western Hemispheres ended up from a purely Ferguson ancestry, which says much for the original concept of the Ford Ferguson 9N and TE-20 models.

Below: An early production Massey Harris 744PD.

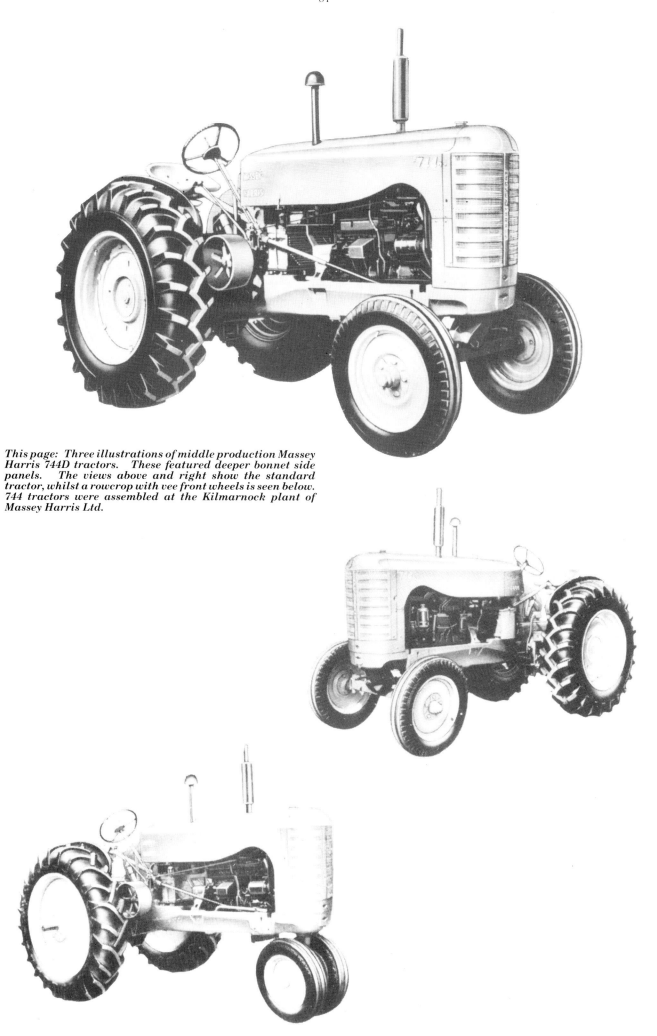

This page: Three illustrations of middle production Massey Harris 744D tractors. These featured deeper bonnet side panels. The views above and right show the standard tractor, whilst a rowcrop with vee front wheels is seen below. 744 tractors were assembled at the Kilmarnock plant of Massey Harris Ltd.

The rowcrop version of the Massey Harris 744. The hydraulic system fitted to this model was vastly inferior to that of the Fergie 20.

A late 744D in Standard form. The P6(TA) engine by Perkins developed 46BHP @ 1350 RPM.

The Perkins L4(TA) engine was fitted to two 744 tractors which were sent to Racine for evaluation, before the introduction of the 745 model.

Above: The final production version of the M-H 745.

Left and Below: The M-H 745S was produced in an attempt to reduce the price of the tractor.   Following numerous failures the frame had to be reinforced as seen in the example below.

Chapter Seven
Post Merger Developments

A more powerful version of the TO-20, as the equivalent model was called in the USA, actually came in August 1951 with the fitting of a larger Continental Z-129 unit, but unlike the English equivalent, the model was redesignated the TO-30.

It was in 1954 that the TO-35 with even larger bore in its engine came onto the Western Hemisphere market. This tractor also featured a six speed gearbox and improved hyraulics, with position control fitted. Production at Ferguson's Dearborn plant never reached that of Banner Lane, in fact by the end of the TE-20 in 1956 Coventry had built 517651 units and Dearborn only 169000.

Now under Massey Harris control, in effect, although the merger of 1953 was an effective takeover in real terms, it was 1956 before a new model came in the United Kingdom. The TO35 came onto a market where a 'two line' policy was operated in the Western Hemisphere, with Massey Harris models continuing in production for sale through former Massey dealers, and Ferguson for sale through Ferguson dealers.

After the merger, in the United Kingdom, where dealer structures were somewhat different, many Massey Harris dealers found themselves selling Ferguson tractors after 1954. You had the situation where some dealers sold Fordson tractors and Massey Harris implements - there were not that many M-H tractors sold in the UK anyway! Changes in the Ford policy regarding dealers, with a move away from their car and truck dealers selling tractors unknowingly helped some dealers to change to 'grey'.

The late 1956 introduction of the FE-35 brought this new model onto the UK market later than anticipated. Unlike its US counterpart, the TO-35 the tractor featured revised styling, and instead of a tilting bonnet it had a service flap to gain access to the fuel tank(s).

The TVO and Petrol engines were now of 87mm bore and were rated at 30/34hp. The diesel had the new 23C engine which now had a bore of 84.14mm and was rated at 37hp @ 2000rpm. In due course a dual clutch and 'live' PTO were optional.

Finished in a grey and gold colour scheme the new model looked very smart, but the diesel version soon gained a reputation for being a bad starter; Harry Ricardo had been brought in to improve the engine and it seemed that the 'improvements' had a detrimental effect!

The Massey Ferguson hierarchy were none too happy that the Banner Lane plant was not in their ownership. Protracted negotiations started in 1957 to take over the plant; this did not involve the engine production facility.

It so happened around that time that F. Perkins Ltd., of Peterborough were passing through less fortunate times. The onslaught of 'own make' diesels, coupled with the success of Ford's new 590E and 592E engines, plus the drying up of the conversion pack market was taking its toll on sales.

Still a family concern in effect, Massey Ferguson had the opportunity of obtaining capacity to supply diesel engines for both Eastern and Western Hemisphere operations on acquisition of the plant. Until that time, US tractors had used Continental Diesels.

By 1958/9, both Banner Lane and the Peterborough plant of F. Perkins were under MF control.

Faced with a drying up of sales for its engines, the Standard Motor Co. even considered building its own tractors; indeed prototypes were even built. The planned range of implements and the tractor never came to anything - New Idea were to be involved but in the end Standard had to be content in selling their 23C engines to Allis Chalmers for the ED40. They continued to supply petrol engines to MF, and also to Ford for their Dexta.

Perkins had successfully updated their P3 engine for Ford to be used in the Dexta, and at the same time took the opportunity of revising their own production unit. The result was the P3/144, a development of which very soon found its way into the Ferguson 35 as the P3/152.

Gone were the cold starting problems associated with the 23C engine and the 35 settled down to a successful run which lasted until it was superseded by the 135 in 1965. During that time further improvements were made. 'Live' Hydraulics and PTO also made their appearance, and from 1962 the 35X with more powerful Perkins A3/152 engine was introduced. Even after Perkins came under M-F control, engines were still supplied to Ford for both the Dexta, Super Dexta, and other applications; indeed other tractor manufacturers as well still fitted Perkins.

We now have to go back in time to discuss the introduction of a larger tractor. It is well known that Harry Ferguson was opposed to large tractors, yet by 1950 he was beginning to realise that the only way into the growing world market was to build a bigger machine.

The experimental and design departments at Fletchamstead, Coventry, in anticipation of the forthcoming merger with Massey Harris, began work on a larger tractor, and some six prototypes were assembled between 1952 and 1956.

The engine was designed by Polish Engineer Alec Senkowski and was so arranged that it could have 2,3,4 or 6 cylinders and could be built for petrol, diesel, or TVO operation. About a dozen engine blocks were cast; it is not known how many were built up. Most of the extant photographs show a tractor with a petrol engine designated the 45C. If volume production had been attained the tractor would have been designated the TE-60. After it was realised that the '45' engines would prove very expensive to produce, a Perkins L4 was tried in one of the tractors. The original TE-20 design showed weaknesses in the rear axle which were never overcome. The LTX used a double reduction rear axle design to reduce the load on the crown wheel and differential.

Once Massey Harris had a hand in the affair, the larger end of the market, was, in effect, covered by the 744 and 745 models. But as we have seen elsewhere these were not doing too well as far as sales were concerned.

The cost of putting the LTX into production was prohibitive, so Massey Ferguson, as it became in due course, looked elsewhere for a means of bringing a tractor to compete with the Fordson Major, Nuffield Universal Four, and International BWD6 onto the UK market.

It so happened, that after the merger, Massey Harris dealers in the USA, mainly due to the unpopularity of the then current M-H range, asked for a Masseyised Fergie.

The result was the Massey Harris 50, which was simply a Ferguson TO-35 altered to provide a rowcrop beam style front axle, which could also be replaced by a single front wheel or vee twin wheels, increased ground clearance, and provided with Massey Harris style tinwork.

There was a resultant backlash from the Fergie dealers in the USA to this model, and the Ferguson 40 was created in 1956. The tractor was 'deMasseyised' with distinctive new tinwork and sold through the Ferguson dealers.

The 'two line' dealer policy was phased out in 1957 and the need for two different models subsided.

By fitting the Perkins 4.192 engine to the Massey Harris 50 carcass the Massey Ferguson Dieselmatic 65 was introduced in the USA. Frontal styling was 'halfway' between Ferguson and M-H tradition. In fact, apart from the improved gearbox there was little more to this machine than the Ford Ferguson 9NAN into which Frank Perkins fitted a P4 for his own use during the War. It took another ten years or so for the power to be applied to basically the same transmission.

To provide the UK with a similar tractor, the press tools for the 40 tinwork were shipped to the Banner Lane plant, and thus the 65 in Britain took on the appearance of the erstwhile Ferguson 40, with important differences.

Double reduction hubs were provided at the end of the axle shafts and disc brakes fitted.

Later 65s received the Perkins AD4.203 engine which was now direct injection and developed 58.38hp @ 2000 rpm. The original engine put out 50.5hp.

A final feature of late series 35 and 65 tractors was 'Multipower'. This doubled the number of working speeds. A hydraulically operated high/low range with on the move shift capability was fitted ahead of the main transmission train. A separate hydraulic pump, mounted on top of the main tractor hydraulic pump in the rear transmission, provided the power source. One design flaw was that engine braking was not available in low range - a weakness which the author of this book found to his cost on one occasion.

Industrial models of both the 35 and 65 were produced, and these had the option of torque convertor transmission. The 35 was also produced in Vineyard form, with a diesel engine avilable on this model for the first time.

Below: A publicity shot taken at Stoneleigh when the two line policy was still very much in vogue in the USA. Fergie 35s and Massey Harris 745s appear with M-F combines.

The 35 was available in petrol/TVO form and the model was still available in the late fifties.

The original 35 was finished in a grey and gold livery and featured new styling. The diesel engined variant is seen right and below, and this used the Standard 23C diesel.

Above: Ferguson tractors were always popular with industrial and public works users. Here is a TVO 35 fitted with road tyres and fenders, and front bumper.

Below and Right: A vineyard model of the MF 35 was available with a minimum track width of 32" and overall width of 46". Fitted with 9.00 x24" rear and 5.00 x 15" rear tyres an lower profile as attained, with 10" instead of 12.25" ground clearance. A diesel model was introduced, this being the first Ferguson vineyard model to feature a c.i. engine. Note the problem of the additional batteries required for starting; these are mounted untidily on either side of the clutch housing, but are not evident on the TVO model shown to the right.

Above: Negotiations were in hand during 1958 for the purchase of the Banner Lane factory from the Standard Motor Co., and this took effect from 31st August 1959. The first tractor under new ownership was driven off the line by Clifford Bass, during the night shift. Note the adoption of red and grey livery and Massey Ferguson decals. Massey Harris Ferguson, born from the merger in 1954, became Massey Ferguson in 1958.

Left: A Vineyard MF 35 at work.

Below: Baling using a MF 35 and Massey Ferguson PTO driven baler.

Chapter Eight
Perkins Diesels

With Ford and Nuffield offering Perkins engined variants, and David Brown their own diesel engine, it was not long before Ferguson's sales force were calling for a diesel version of the TE-20. Now as Harry Ferguson himself was not a diesel fan, it took some considerable persuasion to get him to agree to a diesel engined tractor at all.

The Perkins P3 was looked at, but the cost of installation and the modifications needed would not suit, so a Standard engine was fitted instead.

There was one thing which opened the way for a conversion pack from Perkins for the Fergie 20 and that was the fact that the diesel engine supplied by Ferguson could not be fitted to existing tractors. The first tractor converted by Perkins was actually a Ford-Ferguson 9NAN for his own use, but the principles of the conversion were the same for the TE-20, apart from the fact that Perkins used an early version of the P4 engine.

When Massey Harris were looking at building tractors in the UK, a few type 44 frames were taken and fitted with the P6(TA) engine, at Peterborough. The P6 engine was chosen for production of the 744 as it became.

Thus, not only were Perkins engines now being fitted in production by leading manufacturers, they were also available to convert s.i. engined units to diesel. By the late forties 'conversion packs' were available to convert the lions share of popular models.

The promotion of Diesel conversion packs was just as well, as new engine business fell off considerably with Ford fitting their own diesel to the New Fordson Major, and Nuffield fitting the BMC engine to the Universal by the early fifties.

1953 saw the introduction of a completely new engine for industrial use - the L4. The removal of a Continental HD260 diesel from one of the 44s sent over from the U.S.A. for development purposes saw this engine being dismantled at Peterborough, and some ideas from the same were incorporated in the L4 engine. This unit was designed expressly for low speeds up to 2000rpm. It had a bore and stroke of 4.25 x 4.75", a swept volume of 4.42 litres, and could be set to give up to 59bhp @ 2000rpm. A gear driven timing arrangement was fitted and the camshaft, unlike the P series, was in the normal position with push rod operation of the valves. The cylinder liners were, however, of the wet type.

The new engine was adopted by various manufacturers for use in tractors. The Massey Harris 745 used the L4(TA) from 1953, and M-H also adopted it for their combines. Just to confuse th issue the development tractors were 744 with the new L4 engine fitted!

There was however a development version of the P3 which had a simple gear driven timing train and a small Holburn-Eaton type oil pump driven from underneath the crankshaft timing gear. This allowed the CAV in-line injection pump to be flange mounted directly onto the back of the timing case. All external oil and water pipes were eliminated. It was called the P3.144 and eliminated the expensive features of the P3, the skew driven oil pump, and the chain driven timing. Four cylinder (P4.192) and six cylinder (P6.288) variants were also built.

In the early 'sixties the cylinder bores of the P3/144 were opened up to 3.6" diameter in common with other engines in the P series. A C.A.V. DPA fuel injection pump was fitted and the engine became the 3.152.

Perkins became part of Massey Ferguson Limited in 1959, and this consolidated the use of Perkins products in MF tractors. In fact from 31st August 1959 Massey Ferguson had taken over the Banner Lane Coventry plant of the Standard Motor Co. This did not involve any engine manufacture, and M-F were keen to move to a stage where their new subsidiary would provide all the engines for the tractor plant. The Standard 23C engine had a reputation as a bad starter, especially in cold weather.

The first Perkins engines used in a Massey Ferguson (as opposed to a Massey Harris) tractor were fitted in the new M-F 65 tractor introduced in 1958. The Perkins 4.192 engine was chosen to power this tractor and this gave the UK market a 50HP plus tractor with the Ferguson System which put the competition in the shade somewhat.

Shortly after the M-F control of Banner Lane took effect, the M-F 35 was given a three cylinder Perkins 3.152 engine.

In 1961, a direct injection version of the 4.192 engine, which in its bored out form to 3.6" was the 4.203, came into production, and this was known as the AD-4.203. This was used in the M-F 65 from its inception.

With the Fordson Super Dexta on the market, ironically with engines from Perkins, the 35 was given the A3.152 engine from 1962. Perkins also supplied A3.152 engines for Ferguson's Detroit plant which were fitted to MF35s there, and also MF50 tractors. The Dieselmatic 65 used the 4A.203 engine in the USA, and later the AD4.203, whilst the Super 90, only built in the Western Hemisphere used new unit called the A4.300.

The 4.270 was an update on the old L4 engine, and brought direct injection to this engine, plus the use of a distributor type fuel injection pump.

Now that Perkins was part of MF, the production facility at Peterborough was used to develop and build most of the engines in future MF tractors, yet many of the engines used in the tractors described in the last chapters of this book were existing designs, or developments of them.

Full details of engines supplied by F. Perkins Ltd., to other manufacturers and for conversions can be found in the book "Vintage Tractor Special - 8; Perkins Diesel Conversions & Factory Fitted Units", from this publisher.

Above: Many readers may not realise that the predecessor of the MF65 really appeared during the War. Frank Perkins of Peterborough fitted a Ford Ferguson 9NAN with a Perkins P4 engine.

Below: The Perkins P3(TA) was adapted for use as a conversion pack for the Fergie 20. The original conversion is seen here. The engine was an Engineering dept. prototype and used standard Mark III P series parts, which included the high position water pump, large oil filter and P4 vehicle exhaust manifold.

The final version of the P3(TA) conversion pack is seen here at work. The engine developed 34BHP @ 2000rpm which was a useful increase over the normal tractor.

Above: The conversion required the use of a higher bonnet line because of the higher profile of the engine.

Left and Below: The installation in progress is seen here. The use of a redesigned water pump and simplified exhaust manifold lowered the bonnet line and also reduced cost!

This 35 was fitted with a Perkins P3(TA) engine for development purposes. When a Perkins engine was finally adopted, it was the P3.152 engine that was used as seen below, left and right. This development of the P3 was of 3.6" bore and 5" stroke and ran at 2200RPM to give a 33/37HP rating, and featured gear driven timing. The 35 fitted with such an engine is seen (bottom), posed at the MF training school at Stoneleigh.

*Above: The 35X featured a more powerful version of the Perkins 3-152 engine, the A3-152, and was produced from 1962.
Although production of the 35 ceased in the UK in 1964, assembly continued elsewhere.   The shot below is most likely of a French
built machine.*

A Perkins powered MF 35 ploughing with a three furrow plough.

A 35 at work on a French farm with a French built MF 825 in the background.

With the end of the two line policy in 1958 the Massey Harris 50 and Ferguson 40 models had become the Massey Harris 50, with unified styling for the Western Hemisphere and whilst a Continental petrol engine was offered, so was the Perkins A3-152 diesel. Note the power shift rear wheels.

Below: With the disposal of tooling and patterns to Industrija Masina Traktora of Beograd, Yugoslavia, this concern began to produce the old 35 as the IMT 539. Some of these were sold in the UK in the early 'eighties. The anti-roll bar was to comply with current UK safety requirements, and the forward directed exhaust kept noise levels for the driver under the legal limit. 35s were also built in India. The Perkins engines, were, of course, built under licence.

One of the six LTX prototypes. In appearance it was very much a 'grown up' TE-20.

Below and below left: Some of the prototypes lasted for quite some time due to their robustness and good design.

The prototype shown here had a 4 cylinder petrol engine designated the 45C.

The 45C engined LTX with bonnet raised to show the rear mounted fuel tank. Another prototype was fitted with an L4(TA) engine from Perkins.

Above and Below: An LTX prototype was dressed up with a new bonnet to match current UK Fergie 35 styling. The view below is taken for comparison with the then current Massey Harris 50 model sold in the USA and Canada.

The MF 65 was the Massey Ferguson response to the need for a tractor in the 50HP class to compete with Ford and Nuffield. Following the realisation that the LTX prototypes would cost too much to put into production, the Western Hemisphere practice of modifying the existing model to suit was adopted. The 35 transmission was taken, and given epicyclic final reduction gearing on the outer ends of the rear axle shafts, and a Perkins 4.192 diesel was fitted. Front axle and front end were pure Ferguson 40/ Massey Harris 50, and to save on costs the press tools for the 40 tinwork, (now out of production) were shipped to the UK and the 65 given its distinctive styling. The final reduction gearing was to compensate for increase in wheel size and increased engine power; the existing gearbox being able to absorb the increased torque at higher speeds. Disc brakes were fitted, and the abandonment of the Ferguson style front axle allowed for the fitting of a single front wheel or vee twin wheels where necessary.

The UK built 65 tractors in their red and grey finish looked a deal smarter than the same styled Ferguson 40 tractors.

The MF 65 Dieselmatic sold in the USA had a different styling and the example seen here also has 'power shift' rear wheels.

Bottom: A 65, seen with matching MF trailer, is seen equipped with front wheel weights. The later Perkins AD4.203 engine developed 58.38HP @ 2000RPM.

Above; Also available were the 65R and 65S industrial models. Whilst the 65S had a normal dual clutch transmission, the 65R had an 11.75" Borg & Beck Torque Convertor and a shuttle transmission which gave four speeds in each direction. A diff. lock and handbrake were optional, as was a crankshaft hydraulic pump to operate loading shovels, etc. Power assisted steering was also available.

Below: The M-F Super 90 was only sold in the Western Hemisphere. This featured either a Continental E242 Gasoline engine or the Perkins A4-300 unit seen here. This was the first engine developed specially for tractor use by Perkins following the M-F takeover. An eight or sixteen speed shift-on-the-go transmission was employed and this model replaced the 85 which had been produced in 1958.

Above: This Fergie 20 was fitted with a Perkins 4.99 engine as the development tractor for the French built M-F 30 which can be seen below. This little tractor used the uprated version of the 4.99, the 4.107, and became the 130 in 1965. Its intention was to provide a small tractor for the French market, where many small farmers still used motor cultivators. In true French style, our example here is seen complete with fore end loader and mounted mower.

Seen here outside the Ferguson HQ at Fletchampstead are two of the TE-20s modified for the Antarctic expedition. On January 4th 1958 Sir Edmund Hillary reached the South Pole with 3 Ferguson petrol tractors after a three month, 1200 mile journey reaching a height of 10000 feet and in temperatures likely to reach -30 degrees F. This must have been the ultimate test for the little Fergies, which were standard models with minor modifications, e.g. heavy duty batteries, starter and wiring, plus various tracks. During the 1200 mile journey an Army 'Weasel' accompanied them but had to be abandoned after numerous breakdowns. The engines had to be adjusted to run at 3000 rpm. On reaching the South Pole, Sir Edmund Hillary arranged for a telegram to be sent to the Ferguson factory in Coventry saying how pleased he was with the tractors. The first task for the tractors on arrival was to assist in unloading supplies (below)

Above: This shot gives an impression of what conditions were like on the journey.

Right: The faithful 'Fergie' takes a breather while its driver has a look out on the bleak landscape.

Below: back from the ordeal, the '20' that went to the South Pole reposes for all to see in the Ferguson museum at Banner Lane.

Above and below: The Tracpak was produced by a Leeds firm from early 1952 and several hundred appear to have been sold. The Sales leaflet stated that the conversion could be fitted in an hour and fifteen minutes and back to wheels in less than an hour. The illustration below shows the Perkins P3(TA) conversion to advantage.

Opposite Page: Top: This conversion was undertaken by a Mr. Burdge of Yatton, and used the tracks and sprockets from an ex army 'Weasel'. The conversion took about three hours and was designed to enable the tractor to be used as a four wheeled machine in summer and a tracked machine in winter. One problem was the steering, because the independent brakes were retained and were not really big enough for the job.

Centre: These tracks were marketed by H. Cameron Gardner Ltd., again with the quick emphasis on conversion from normal wheeled equipment.

Bottom: A 4WD conversion by Selene SAS of Italy carried out by Reekie Brothers in Scotland.

Chapter Nine
The Ferguson Combine

In the forties and early fifties just about every manufacturer of implements in the UK was designing machines to fit the Fergie 20. In addition to this Ferguson themselves were working on various machines

to use the TE-20 as a power unit. A "Wrap round" baler was developed in the USA, and in the U.K. this combine was produced.

The whole ensemble 'wrapped around' a TE-20 which itself had to be modified by virtue of the attachment of mounting brackets onto it, and the widening of the nearside track.

Whilst the machine itself operated successfully, the development costs were high, and with the merger in 1954, Massey Harris had other ideas about combines and the project was dropped.

Right: The tractor unit about to back under the combine which, when out of use was supported on two brackets whose posts were dug in the ground.

Below: The combine in section.

Left: The Combine on the forecourt at Fletchampstead.

Right: From this angle it was easy to mistake the unit for any small self propelled combine.

Left: The unit was, naturally, turned out as a bagger as this was the way in which grain was handled in the 1950s.

Right: The combine at work. Note the relocation of the tractor batteries.

Ferguson Factories.

Top: Banner Lane Coventry, in Standard Motor Co. Days.

Right: Banner Lane in MF days with the tower block prominent.

Below: The Fletchampstead Highway premises of Harry Ferguson Ltd., long before the surrounding area was built up.

Bottom: The Detroit premises of Harry Ferguson Inc.

Above: Banner Lane in Fergie 20 days when Continental engines were still being used. The tractor in the foreground is about to have its wheels and bonnet fitted.

Below: FE35 tractors on the line in the days of the Standard 23C engine.

Banner Lane in the MF era. Left: Perkins engined MF-35s are assembled. Below: MF-35s roll of the line in the days between 1958 and 1959 when the Standard 23C engine was fitted.

A Massey Ferguson 65 is given a running test at the end of the production line. It is followed by what seems to be an endless line of 35s.

Above: Banner Lane in the days of the 100 series, with 135 tractors being assembled.

Below: The French plant with M-F 30s coming off the line.

Chapter Ten
New Designs for the Sixties

By the early sixties, there was indeed a certain amount of standardisation in the MF tractors built in both Eastern and Western Hemispheres, unlike Fords, for example, whose designs in England and the USA were totally different.

With the trend towards unified product lines moving ahead in all automotive fields, MF took the step to introduce a completely new range of models in 1965, with unified styling and specifications worldwide. The demand for Gasoline engines was still evident in the USA, and thus Continental engines still appeared in these tractors.

The MF135 replaced the 35., the MF150 the MF50 (available only in the Western hemisphere), and the 165 the 65. In fact these models bore a similar relationship to each other as the 35-50-65 did. The use of Perkins engines saw the MF135 and MF150 fitted with the AD3.152 engine, the MF165 had the AD4.203 of its predecessor. Whilst Continental engines were still available in all these models, the Z134 in the 135 Special, the Z145 in the MF135 deluxe, and MF150, and the G176 in the MF165, Petrol versions of the Perkins engines were developed and the later MF135/MF150 became available with the Perkins AG3.152 engine and the 165 with the AG4.212. Six forward speeds were provided in all models along with two reverse, but the equipping of any model with "Multipower" doubled those. The 135 retained the beam type front axle of its predecessor, whilst the other models had the usual arrangement to allow the use of row crop type equipment. All models had a new styling with "squared up" appearance.

The 175 was a new model, and featured a Perkins 4.236 engine. This was designed specially to fit the tractor, and was the first Perkins engine to feature the inlet and exhaust manifolds on the same side. Indeed, when the 165 was updated in 1968 to become the 168, the old style AD4.203 engine had given way to a new unit based on the 4.236 but with shorter stroke, the 4.212. The American built 180 was similar but designed for rowcrop work.

The 100 series actually continued in production until 1979, being gradually overtaken by the 200 series. Full details of actual production dates can be found in the serial number tables at the back of this book. The first updates announced were a power boost for the 165 and the 175 which became the 178.

The first cabs made available for the 100 series were not safety cabs, indeed they were constructed of fibreglass. The first safety cabs were of composite construction with canvas (plastic) infill, and the option of engine side shrouds which diverted engine heat to warm the cab. In due course full safety cabs to 'Q' specification had to be supplied for UK use, but as the 100 series were being produced mainly for overseas markets by the mid seventies, it was often the case that domestic sales received proprietory cabs.

One of the problems when a cab was fitted was the restricted access to the driving position. This was overcome by introducing a spacer on the 100 series from late 1971, which fitted between the gearbox and rear axle and lengthened the wheelbase of the tractor. This allowed the fitting of a more spacious safety cab. It also altered the weight distribution of the tractor to advantage, allowing the attachment and use of heavier implements without the need for front weights. With these improvements, including the use of spacers, the 135 became the 148, the 165 became the 168, the 135 the 148, and the 185, which had been introduced to replace the 178 in June 1971. The 1971 range still included the 135 and 165 however, and a stretched version of the 185, the 188 was also introduced, in time for Smithfield Show in 1971, where the improved range were shown. But the spacer idea was also put to good use in using the space for an optional 'creeper' gearbox in place of the spacer. As far as normal gearboxes were concerned, the 130 had an eight speed gearbox within high and low ratios, whilst the other models had a basic six speed transmission over high and low ratios, which became 12 with the application of 'Multipower', which was optional.

The smallest model sold in the UK was the 130, which was an update of the MF30 built in France, with a Perkins 4.107 four cylinder diesel. On the other hand, the largest conventional tractor available on world markets was the US built 1100, fitted with the Perkins A6.354 diesel or a Waukesha F320-G six cylinder petrol engine. This became the 1130 when fitted with a turbocharged version of the diesel engine, the Perkins AT6.354. The 1080 was a relative, but this had a Perkins 4.318 diesel. The ultimate in 100 series power was the 1150 built at the Detroit plant from 1970-72, which featured a Perkins V8.510 diesel.

The story continues with the introduction of the 200 series and the big four wheel drive models in the seventies. They are too recent history to find a place in this book, but no doubt as time passes future editions will encompass them.

Farming in the 1970s was rapidly becoming more sophisticated, more mechanised, and more commercial. Yet there was still a need for basic tractors to bring the third world into the era of mechanisation. The dream of Harry Ferguson, with farming mechanised worldwide using the Ferguson System continues to become more of a reality.

The smallest tractor in the 100 range was the French built 130. It was little different from the 825 which it replaced. It had the Perkins 4.107 engine which developed 26.96/23.06BHP, and retained the eight speed gearbox.

The 135 was the successor to the 35, using the Perkins 3.152 engine.   The diesel version is seen above, whilst the Petrol engined tractor is seen below.   The 135 became the 148 with the fitment of a spacer.

Above: Whilst the MF 135 built in the United Kingdom was originally turned out with a Standard 87mm engine, the majority of the petrol tractors sold were assembled in the USA, and had Continental Z-134. Later on, the petrol tractors were turned out with a new petrol engine from Perkins, the AG3.152. A small number of petrol engined demonstrators were kept in the UK for loan to Show Jumping events where they did not have the noise of the diesels to disturb the horses.

Right: The original cab fitted to the 135 was made in Glass Reinforced Plastic.

Right and below: The 135 was eventually available with the square topped fenders used on the larger models.

Left and above: late 135s had a revised front axle design, and improved engine with new type injection pump.

The 135S was designed for Industrial applications, and could be finished in an alternative yellow and grey colour scheme. The example shown is fitted with the spacer to lengthen the wheelbase.

A celebration was held to mark the 21st anniversary of tractor production at Banner Lane. Left: Alex Patterson, Jimmy Jones, and Alan Botwood pose with Ferguson TE-20 number one, and in the lower shots a brand new 135, successor to the 20, is driven off the line by Works Manager, Jimmy Jones.

The 165 was produced from 1965 to 1968 when it became the 168.

The 165 came out originally with the old style AD4.203 engine. The updated version shown right and below which in due course became the 168 received the new version of this engine which was based on the 4.236 engine, and classified 4.212. It had the same bore as the 4.236 but a shorter stroke at 4.5"

The 175 was the largest model to be sold in the UK. The Perkins 4.236 engine gave 63.34/55.69 BHP.

Another view of the later 175 tractor. All 100 series models sold in the UK other than the 130 were available with the usual six speed (three high/three low) transmission but the application of Multipower doubled this.

The 168 replaced the 165 in 1971. The example shown here features the improved seat, increased engine power, and the use of the spacer to lengthen the wheelbase.

The 178 replaced the 175 in 1968.   The example shown to the left shows the spacer with which these models were equipped to give more room for fitment of a cab.

The 188 was phased in to supersede the 178 from 1971/2. Note the front wheel weights and 'power shift' rear wheels on this example.

Cabs are on display in these posed shots taken at Stareton. The idea of the engine side sheets was to collect warm air from the engine and use it to heat the inside of the cab in cold weather.

The big 1100 was assembled in the USA, and was introduced in 1965. It was not sold in the UK at that time. Using the Perkins 6.354 engine, it developed into the 1130, introduced in 1966, which used a turbocharged version of the same engine.

Below: Continual development takes place with M-F products, and tractors are specially assembled for test purposes. Here is an example of such a machine involved in development work.

Chapter 11
Grey was the Colour!

It is well known that the Ferguson system was first shown to the world at large in a battleship grey colour scheme.

This was, however, not the original intention of Harry Ferguson, as his prototype tractor was painted black. When it came to production, his design team persuaded him to adopt a 'less austere' colour, and grey was chosen.

A single colour of course helped to keep costs down, and in the United Kingdom there was not much of a panache for extravagant liveries as far as tractors were concerned.

It came therefore, as no surprise, that when launched into the US market in 1939, the good old battleship grey was adopted for the 9N. Somewhat dull one may consider alongside the 'Persian orange', 'Flambeau red', and other exotic schemes used to adorn the other US manufacturers' products in the streamline era.

This colour became the norm for all Fergusons for the next ten years or so, and the British built TE-20 gained the nickname of 'the grey menace' when it appeared like mushrooms in the farmyards of Britain, much to the chagrin of the Ford and other salesmen.

The Massey Harris merger did not affect the colour scheme of Ferguson origin equipment at first. However, the introduction of new models in the USA gave the incentive to give these a special identity. As styling in the Western Hemisphere remained firmly allied to the 'TO-20' the adoption of a beige and metallic green livery for the TO-35 gave it a distinctive appearance. These colours were especially chosen to contrast with the then current Ford red and grey.

The introduction of the 35 in the Eastern Hemisphere saw new styling and it was allied to a new colour scheme. The new tractor was finished in a grey and gold livery. This was arrived at after having painted tractors in every conceivable colour for evaluation - the chance arrival of a paint representative from Pinchin & Johnston at Fletchampstead produced the copper paint, and grey tinwork was added to the tractor. Parked away from the rest of the evaluation tractors it drew the attention of the management team in the sunlight, and the colour was adopted. Unfortunately Banner Lane used a different paint supplier and were never able to get the gloss of the first example. Gold was also used by Massey Harris in the USA for the 50, with red bonnet, whilst Ferguson marketed tractors remained beige and metallic green until the two line policy went and the new red and grey colours were adopted universally. The grey was much more of a metallic shade in the Western Hemisphere, and this was reflected when the new 'Worldwide' 100 series took over in 1964-5.

Other manufacturers tried to combat the success of the Ferguson tractor, especially the TE-20. Whilst it is true that the Ford 8N, whose sheer numbers in the USA eclipsed what Ferguson was able to produce, accounted for some 10 times the production of the equivalent Ferguson TO-20, in the United Kingdom the 'Grey Menace' and its sales created a thorn in the side of the other manufacturers. Fordson fought back with their Dexta, based firmly on the 9N/8N concept but with Perkins built diesel engine. International introduced the B250, the first wholly Doncaster designed project, and BMC launched their Mini Tractor, ably assisted by design staff recruited from Ferguson. Allis Chalmers tried to update their 'torque tube technology' with the D272 and ED40 models. It was just as well that the Standard tractor, born out of the loss of Banner Lane to M-F, did not materialise.

In the world of the nineteen-nineties the 'Grey Fergie' is still to be seen in number. There are many still in use on small farms and smallholdings through the length and breadth of the United Kingdom, and in many overseas territories. On the other hand, many examples are being purchased for preservation and can be seen at rallies and shows. The Ferguson 'mania' now extends to implements, and there are those who are trying to collect every variety shown in this book to attach to their 'Fergie'.

The world moves on, and agriculture must in itself prepare for the twenty first century. That need is being met by the current products of M-F, whether they be the latest 'hi-tech' models for the European arable farmer, or a basic tractor for the developing third world. It is right therefore that what can be seen coming out of Banner Lane in the 'nineties can be justly proud of its ancestry in 'The wee grey Fergie'.

Ferguson and Massey Ferguson Tractor Engine Specifications

Make	Cyls	Bore x Stroke	CC.	Fuel	HP	Used in.
C. Climax/D.B.	4	3.125" x 4"	2010	G/K	20	Type 'A'
Ford	4	3.187" x 3.75"	1966	G/K	23.87	9N/2N/9NAN.
Cont. Z-120	4	81mm x 95mm	1966	G.	23.9	TE-20/TO-20(1)
Standard	4	80mm x 92mm	1850	G. G/K	23.9	TEA-20 etc.(2)
Standard	4	85mm x 92mm	2088	G. G/K	28.2	TEA-20 etc.(3)
Cont. Z-129	4	3.25" x 3.875"	2113	G.	30.27	TO-30 (4)
Cont. Z-134	4	3.3125" x 3.875"	2195	G.	32.80	TO-35, F-40, (5)
Standard	4	80.96mm x101.6mm	2092	D.	26.00	TEF-20 (6)
Perkins P3(TA)	3	3.5" x 5"	2360	D.	34.00	Conversion pack.
Perkins P6(TA)	6	3.5" x 5"	4730	D.	46.00	MH 744.
Perkins L4(TA)	4	4.25 x 4.75"	4420	D.	50.00	MH 745
Standard	4	87mm x 92mm	2186	G. G/K	34.00	FE 35, 135 Petrol.
Standard 23C	4	84.14 x 101.6mm	2258	D.	34.00	FE 35,
Perkins 4A-203	4	3.6" x 5".	3335	D.	55.50	MF 65
Perkins 3.152	3	3.6" x 5".	2489	D.	35.00	MF 35, MF 50.
Perkins A3-152	3	3.6" x 5"	2500	D.	41.50	MF 35X, MF 50, MF 135
Perkins AD4-203	4	3.6 x 5"	3335	D.	55.50	MF 65. MF 165.
Cont. G 176	4	3.58" x 4.38"	2883	G	46.92	MF 65. (W.H.) MF 165
Cont. Z 145	4	3.375" x 4.062"	2376	G	35.36	MF 135 D/L, MF 150.
Perkins AG3.152	3	3.6" x 5"	2489	G	35.00	Late MF 135/ MF 150.
Perkins AG4.212	4	3.875" x 4.5"	3472	G	55.00	MF 165.
Perkins A4.212	4	3.875" x 4.5"	3472	D	58.30	late MF 165/168.
Perkins A4.236	4	3.875 x 5"	3865	D	63.34	MF 175.
Perkins A4.248	4	3.980 x 5"	4062	D	68.00	MF 178.
Perkins A4.300	4	4.5" x 4.75"	4950	D	68.00	MF Super 90.
Cont. G 206	4	3.9" x 4.5"	3374	G.	62.33	MF 175, MF 180
Perkins AG4.236	4	3.875" x 5"	3865	G.	62.00	MF 175, MF 180
Perkins 4.107	4	3.125" x 3.5"	1752	D.	26.96	MF 825, MF130.
Perkins A6.354	6	3.875" x 5"	5798	D.	93.94	MF1100
Perkins AT6.354	6	3.875" x 5"	5798	TD.	120.51	MF1130
Waukesha F320-G	6	4.125" x 4"	5341	G.	90.29	MF1100

Notes: G=Gasoline. G/K= Petrol/TVO. D=Diesel. TD=Turbocharged Diesel.
The numbers in brackets ( ) refer to the list of model codes below.

FERGUSON MODEL DESIGNATIONS

Type A.	David Brown built tractors 1936-7.
9N	Ford built tractors 1939-41
9NAN	Ford built tractors with V.O. engine for U.K. 1939-41
2N	Ford built utility model 1942-45
2NAN	Ford built utility model with V.O. engine for U.K. 1942-45.
TE-20	Standard built tractor with Continental Z-120 engine, 1946-48 (1)
TEA-20	Standard built tractor with Standard engine, petrol. 1947-56 (2) (3).
TO-20	Detroit built tractor with Continental Z-120 engine 1948-31 (1)
TEB-20	Standard built tractor with Continental engine, narrow, 1946-48 (1)
TEC-20	Standard built tractor with Standard engine, narrow, 1948-56 (2) (3).
TED-20	Standard built tractor with V. O. Standard engine, 1949-56 (2) (3).
TEE-20	Standard built tractor with V. O. Standard engine, narrow, 1949-56 (2) (3).
TEF-20	Standard built tractor with Standard diesel engine 1951-56 (6).
TO-30	Detroit built tractor with Continental Z-129 engine, 1951-54 (4)
TEH-20	Standard built tractor with Standard Zero Octane engine 1950-56 (2) (3)
TEJ-20	Standard built tractor with Standard Z.O. engine, narrow, 1950-56. (2) (3).
TEK-20	Standard built tractor with Standard Petrol engine, Vineyard, 1952-56 (3).
TEL-20	Standard built tractor with Standard V.O. engine, Vineyard, 1952-56 (3)
TEM-20	Standard built tractor with Standard Z.O. engine, Vineyard, 1952-56 (3)
TEP-20	Standard built tractor with Standard Petrol engine, Industrial, 1952-56 (3)
TER-20	Standard built tractor with Standard V.O. engine, Industrial, 1952-56 (3)
TES-20	Standard built tractor with Standard Z.O. engine, Industrial, 1952-56 (3)
TET-20	Standard built tractor with Standard Diesel engine, Industrial 1952-56 (6)
TO-35	Detroit built tractor with Continental Z-134 engine, 1954-57. (5)
FE-40	Detroit built tractor with Continental Z-134 engine, 1956-57. (5) Ferguson
MH-50	Detroit built tractor with Continental Z-134 engine, 1955-58 (5) Massey.
FE-35	Standard built tractor with Standard engine 1956-58.
MF-35	Standard/ MF built tractor with Standard engine 1958-59
MF-35	MF built tractor with Perkins 3.152 engine 1959-62.
MF-35X	MF built tractor with Perkins A3-152 engine 1962-64.
MF-65	MF built tractor with Perkins 4.203 engine 1958-65.
MF-25	MF French built tractor with Perkins 4.107 engine 1963-65.
MF-88	MF Detriot built tractor with Continental Diesel 1960-1962.
MF Super 90.	MF Detriot built tractor with Perkins A4.300 engine 1961-1965.
MF-130	MF French built tractor with Perkins 4.107 engine, 1966-72
MF-135	MF built tractor with Perkins A3.152/ Continental Z145/ Perkins AG3.152 engine 1965-79.
MF-148	MF built tractor with Perkins A3.152 engine 1972-1979
MF-150	MF Detroit built tractor with engines as MF-135. 1965-75
MF-165	MF built tractor with Perkins AD4.203 engine 1965-71.
MF-168	MF built tractor with Perkins A4.212 engine 1971-1979.
MF-165	MF built tractor with Perkins A4.212 engine 1971-1979.
MF-175	MF built tractor with Perkins A4.236 engine 1965-1968
MF-180	MF Detriot built tractor with Perkins A4.236 engine 1965-74.
MF-178	MF built tractor with Perkins A4.248 engine 1968-1971
MF-185	MF built tractor with Perkins A4.248 engine 1971-1979
MF-188	MF built tractor with Perkins A4.248 engine 1971-1979
MF-1100	MF Detriot built tractor with Perkins A6.354 engine 1965-72.
MF-1130	MF Detriot built tractor with Perkins AT6.354 engine 1965-72

N.B. Most 100 series tractors sold in the Western Hemisphere were also available with gasoline engines. See engine specification table for details.

SERIAL NUMBERS

Unless indicated, the first serial number in each year is shown.

Ferguson Black Prototype Tractor.

1 only produced 1933.

Ferguson Model 'A' made by David Brown Tractors.

1250 made between 1936 and 1938
1-550 Coventry Climax engine.
551-1350 David Brown engine.

Ford 9N/9NAN/2N/2NAN. with Ferguson System Built Dearborn.

1939	1	1943	107755
1940	14644	1944	131783
1941	47843	1945	174638
1942	92363	1946	204129
		1947	267289
		end	306221

Ferguson TE 20 model made by Standard Motor Company.

1946	1	1952	241336
1947	315	1953	310780
1948	20895	1954	367999
1949	77773	1955	428093
1950	116462	1956	488579
1951	167837	end	517651

TE (Continental) and TEA (Standard) engined tractors
were built side by side up to serial 48000.

85mm engine (Petrol and TVO) cut in at Serial No. 172501 on 22.1.51.

12 Volt Electrics phased in from Serial 250001

Ferguson 35/ Massey Ferguson 35 built at Coventry.

1956	1001	1961	220614
1957	9226	1962	267528
1958	79553	1963	307231
1959	125068	1964	352255
1960	171471	end	388382

Last Standard 23c engine 166595.
First Perkins 3-152 engine 166596

Massey Ferguson 65 Built at Coventry.

1958	500001	1962	551733
1959	510451	1963	552325
1960	520569	1964	593028
1961	533180	end	614024

First A4-203 engine 531453.

Ferguson TO20/ TO30 Built by Harry Ferguson Inc. Detriot.

1948	1	1952	72680
1949	1808	1953	108645
1950	14660	1954	125959
1951	39163	end	140000

TO-30 cut in at Serial No. 60001 in August 1951.

Ferguson TO-35 Built by Massey Harris Ferguson Inc. Detroit.

1954	140001	1956	167157
1955	140006	1957	171741

TO-35 Gas Deluxe.

1958	178216	1960	203680
1959	188851	1961	207427

TO-35 Gas Special.

1958	183348	1960	203198
1959	185504	1961	209484

TO-35 Diesel

1958	180742	1960	203360
1959	187719	1961	203680

Ferguson 40 Built by Massey Harris Ferguson Inc. Detroit.

1956	400001	1957	405671

Massey Harris 50 Built by Massey Harris Ferguson Inc. Detroit.

1955	500001	1957	510764
1956	500473	1958	515708

Following the cessation of the two line policy (F-40 and MH-50 tractors were assembled on the same production line), the model became the MF-50.

Massey Ferguson 135.

1965	101	1969	117429
1966	30283	1970	141426
1967	67597	1971	162200
1968	93305		

Massey Ferguson 135 updated.

1971	400001	1976	457866
1972	403518	1977	469335
1973	419583	1978	479192
1974	432709	1979	487350
1975	445602	end	490714

Massey Ferguson 165.

1965	500001	1969	563701
1966	512207	1970	581457
1967	530825	1971	597745
1968	547384		

Massey Ferguson 165 updated.

1971	100001	1976	145432
1972	103622	1977	155687
1973	116353	1978	164417
1974	126448	1979	173144
1975	135036	end	173696

Massey Ferguson 175 (178 from 1968)

1965	700001	1969	732158
1966	705652	1970	740301
1967	714166	1971	747283
1968	722679	1972	753108

Massey Ferguson 175 S

1968	650000	1971	656011
1969	652061	1972	657362
1970	653721		

Massey Ferguson 148

1972	600001	1977	609159
1973	602153	1978	609969
1974	604449	1979	610893
1975	605578	end	610982
1976	607701		

Massey Ferguson 168

1971	250001	1976	258064
1972	250005	1977	259959
1973	252121	1978	260617
1974	254307	1979	261103
1975	255967	end	261173

Massey Ferguson 185

1971	300001	1976	326109
1972	302833	1977	332107
1973	310398	1978	335211
1974	315219	1979	339755
1975	319923	end	340096

Massey Ferguson 188

1971	350001	1976	365087
1972	350006	1977	368350
1973	353296	1978	370156
1974	357063	1979	371306
1975	360784	end	371333

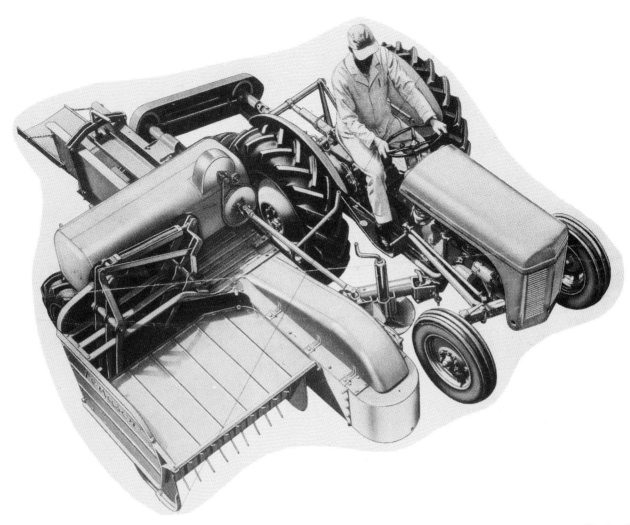

The Ferguson 'Tractor Mate' side mounted baler was developed in Detroit. It succumbed with the end of the 'two line' policy when balers became definitely M-H based. It was also claimed to be the first baler in history that one could convert from twine to wire.